HOW TO PROSPER DURING THE COMING BAD YEARS IN THE 21ST CENTURY

How to Prosper During the Coming Bad Years in the 21st Century

HOWARD J. RUFF

BERKLEY BOOKS, NEW YORK

THE BERKLEY PUBLISHING GROUP
Published by the Penguin Group
Penguin Group (USA) Inc.
375 Hudson Street, New York, New York 10014, USA
Penguin Group (Canada), 90 Eglinton Avenue East, Suite 700, Toronto, Ontario M4P 2Y3, Canada
(a division of Pearson Penguin Canada Inc.)
Penguin Books Ltd., 80 Strand, London WC2R 0RL, England
Penguin Group Ireland, 25 St. Stephen's Green, Dublin 2, Ireland (a division of Penguin Books Ltd.)
Penguin Group (Australia), 250 Camberwell Road, Camberwell, Victoria 3124, Australia
(a division of Pearson Australia Group Pty. Ltd.)
Penguin Books India Pvt. Ltd., 11 Community Centre, Panchsheel Park, New Delhi—110 017, India
Penguin Group (NZ), 67 Apollo Drive, Rosedale, North Shore 0632, New Zealand
(a division of Pearson New Zealand Ltd.)
Penguin Books (South Africa) (Pty.) Ltd., 24 Sturdee Avenue, Rosebank, Johannesburg 2196, South
Africa

Penguin Books Ltd., Registered Offices: 80 Strand, London WC2R 0RL, England

This publication is designed to provide accurate and authoritative information in regard to the subject matter covered. It is sold with the understanding that the publisher is not engaged in rendering legal, accounting, or other professional services. If you require legal advice or other expert assistance, you should seek the services of a competent professional.

While the author has made every effort to provide accurate telephone numbers and Internet addresses at the time of publication, neither the publisher nor the author assumes any responsibility for errors, or for changes that occur after publication. Further, publisher does not have any control over and does not assume any responsibility for author or third-party websites or their content.

PRINTING HISTORY
Berkley trade paperback edition: April 2008

Library of Congress Cataloging-in-Publication Data

Ruff, Howard J.
How to prosper during the coming bad years in the 21st century / Howard J. Ruff.
p. cm.
Rev. ed. of: How to prosper during the coming bad years. 1979.
ISBN 978-0-425-22432-8
1. Finance, Personal. 2. Investments. 3. United States—Economic conditions—21st century. I. Title.

HG179.R78 2008
332.024'01—dc22   2007050588

PRINTED IN THE UNITED STATES OF AMERICA

10 9 8 7 6 5 4 3 2

A great American religious leader once said, "No success in the world can compensate for failure in the home." And when all is said and done (more is said than done), if nothing else I ever do works, if I achieve success in that all-critical area, my life will have been a success.

To this end, I dedicate this book to the following people: my magnificent wife, Kay; our children, and the rest of our posterity; plus my faithful assistant and dear friend, Joann Allen, who has been with me more than twenty-five years and typed every word of several drafts of this book.

This book is also dedicated to my 600,000 newsletter subscribers over the years who have demonstrated their love and appreciation.

Contents

IT'S DÉJÀ VU ALL OVER AGAIN

How to Prosper During the Coming Bad Years was originally published in 1978. I have decided to update it and republish it because the past has come around to haunt us again. The same factors that created the stagflation and the gold and silver bull markets of the late seventies and early eighties are back in spades, and you, as middle class investors, stand to lose just as much as the millions of people who suffered in that era, or bet on the wrong trends.

Rather than write a new book that describes the same situation and tells you the same ways to prepare and profit, I felt it would be easier to create an updated edition of a book that was right on the money thirty years ago, and is again, even more so.

So this book is valuable for today's economic climate. I have eliminated three chapters that are no longer relevant, and I've added three more as a result of having thought about these subjects for thirty years. I'm not getting older; I'm getting smarter.

Take the advice to heart; it really matters. Most of the advice from the seventies is not only just as good today, it's better.

In the late seventies and eighties, economic factors combined to produce a period of inflation and recession unparalleled in our country's history. Those same factors produced the big bull markets for gold and silver, and made people who had the foresight to invest in those areas prosperous, despite the condition of the stock market and the economy. That's when I published the original edition of this book, *How to Prosper During the Coming Bad Years.* I showed people how to prepare for economic hardship and profit in spite of it by investing in gold, silver, and selected commodities and mining stocks.

Unfortunately, those same economic conditions that created the "stagflation" of the seventies and eighties are here again—only this time they're more pronounced. And you as investors stand to lose just as much as people did thirty years ago. With the effects of the real-estate market collapse still rankling through the economy, major businesses reporting billions in losses, and the stock market more volatile than ever, investors today don't know where to turn The government certainly isn't giving you the information you need to know, and neither are your financial advisers.

That's where this book comes in. In the original 1977 edition, I showed people how they could earn money and gain financial stability by making relatively conservative investments in gold and silver. I'm going to do the same thing now—only now I'll tailor my advice specifically to the twenty-first century. To your generation.

This book was originally conceived as a basic text for the hundreds of thousands of subscribers to my financial newsletter, *The Ruff Times,* where I talked and continue to talk in detail about my economic theories. But I believe those principles still hold true today. Some of the material in this book is derived from *The Ruff Times;* some, I've updated from the first edition. But much of the material in this book is totally new, derived from my further studies. That means this book will be useful to longtime *Ruff* subscribers, as well as new readers.

If you want to survive and prosper during the coming bad years—and I believe they're here now or right around the corner—you need this book. You need to know what I have to tell you.

But before I tell you more about your future, let me take you back a few years to where it all began for me.

The Beginning

One day in November 1968, I went to my office to attend a meeting at which I thought I would receive some help and advice from the people who managed the national company with which I owned a speed-reading franchise. I was just beginning to emerge from a very difficult few months, resulting from a prolonged newspaper strike that hit without warning and prevented my company from advertising during our peak months. We had been in financial trouble for some time, but things had started to improve.

When I walked out of that meeting though, my franchise was cancelled and I was wiped out. The struggle to save my company was over. I went to work rich (I thought) and came home broke. My business was down the tubes. My bank had been notified and my accounts were frozen. I had $11.36 in my pocket. I had no money, no job, and no unemployment insurance, because, at the time, there wasn't any such thing for small businessmen. My rather spectacular collapse hit the front pages of the financial sections of the San Francisco Bay Area papers, and I was invited to resign from the Oakland Symphony Finance Committee, because I was embarrassing them. It was a terrible period in my life. It was the crowning blow for me and my wife, as it had only been five months since the accidental drowning of our beautiful twenty-one-month-old son, Ivan.

It was in the depths of that despair that a chain of events began that culminated in the first edition of this book. My family and I decided that such pain, public humiliation, and grief had to be put to some positive purpose for others, as well as for ourselves. So I went to work, armed with determination to learn everything I could from that business failure so it would never happen to me again. It was then that I resolved to apply the principles I had learned from a variety of life experiences.

There was my Mormon upbringing, which stressed prudence, old-fashioned values, avoidance of unsound debt, and a kind of pioneer nineteenth-century rugged self-sufficiency. I'm still a practicing Mormon, and I'm going to keep practicing until I get it right, but this book is not a pulpit. I save this for my Sunday school class.

I had spent years in economic studies, and several years as a stockbroker, specializing in hot stocks and municipal bonds, and had learned a lot, including what not to do. My twenty-five years as an actor and professional singer had taught me to be persuasive and effective in the use of language in front of audiences. Another major asset, which I retained from my venture in the speed-reading business, was my personal ability to read and process information rapidly. I can handle most material at about two thousand words a minute, and I have close-to-total recall. In five hours a day of reading, I process vast amounts of written material and run across things most people would never have a chance to get to. Bits and pieces of information click into place that would not have done so had I not covered so much ground in a short time, and I can quickly become a walking encyclopedia on almost anything.

I was determined to someday repay every debt, even though my financial obligations were discharged through the legal process of bankruptcy. (It took me twelve years, but I finally did it, to the surprise of all my creditors).

When the Bible taught the virtues of "a broken heart and a contrite spirit," I believe it meant that people generally do not bring about real change in their lives until they hit rock bottom and face a choice: change your outlook or self-destruct. And from that bottom in my life came the determination, not only to never repeat the same mistakes that had made me vulnerable, but also to help others avoid personal financial difficulties caused by their lack of understanding of the real world. Thus was the birth of my newsletter, *The Ruff Times* in 1975 (which to date has had more than 600,000 subscribers), and the first edition of this book, which sold more than 2.6 million copies.

My basic studies of economics in college (I majored in Music Education, but minored in Economics), all came together in the creation of this book and *The Ruff Times*. However, that business collapse gave me the perspective, the drive, and hopefully, the character to bring me to today, where I can speak with authority from a pretty good long-term track record as a forecaster and adviser. And that is where I am now—the author of this edition of my bestselling book, and still the editor and publisher of *The Ruff Times* newsletter.

We live in rapidly shifting times, and although I believe the principles expressed in this book will hold true in the early-twenty-first century, short-term and intermediate-term trends can change, creating both risks and opportunities, and time tables and tactics can sometimes use adjustment. I wrote a book that can stand alone, but *The Ruff Times* keeps my subscribers apprised of any changes in the economic climate or in my strategy. I do have alternate strategies in the book for these changes in the economic climate.

You may be reading this book sometime after the initial publication in spring 2008, and advice that was valid when it was published may need to be thought through again, as I don't profess eternal infallibility. It can be updated, either through *The Ruff Times,* or if you are carefully analytical, by looking back through all the basic principles in this book and applying them to changing conditions.

Why Did I Write This Book?

Before I was an author, I was a father and husband, and now I'm a grandfather (sixty-nine grandchildren at last count) and great-grandfather. That's still my number one role in life. I love my wife and my family, and they, along with my religion and my economic outlook, form an inseparable whole. I am concerned about the hard times that may be coming, and my family will have to live in that world. I want to prepare them to get through without physical discomfort and with their values intact. I'm working very hard to see that sound principles of ethics, morality, and good economics are passed on to my offspring. I also believe there are great opportunities to make a lot of money. Everything I write is my legacy to them. Of course, I want them to be proud of me, and I want to give them an example they can emulate.

I also believe that my small amount of this world's wealth (someday I may be half as rich as everyone thinks I am) involves a stewardship, and that I have a responsibility to protect it, magnify it, and use it to bless those who need help. I believe that each one of you who takes my advice will create a little pocket of stability and emotional security for yourself that will stand you in good stead in hard times and help "panic-proof" your life. I want to see every family get its debt under control, and make investments that will beat and profit from the inflationary spiral and create social and financial stability for its members.

You are reading this book because you are perceptive enough to sense that something is terribly wrong out there, as home values drop and the mortgage industry oozes blood. You are one of millions of Americans who has a growing sense of unease about the future, and doubts about those who have their hands on the levers of power. The institutions you have always trusted are now giving you a queasy feeling. You are making more money, but you seem to have less, and you suspect all is not well. I congratulate you for your insight. I share your feelings. I love my country, but sometimes I fear and distrust my government.

I believe America is about to undergo its greatest test since the Civil War. I also believe the nation will ultimately survive some very challenging times, and if enough of us do the right things, we may come out of this stronger and richer than we went into it. I doubt if this book will transform the world, even if it sells a zillion copies, but maybe it can change just enough people's attitudes to tip the scales in a close contest.

I also intend to demolish conventional forecasting and financial planning strategies. Those sacred cows are often outdated, inaccurate, Pollyannaish, and unrealistic, and can lead you and this nation into personal and national economic bondage. Those who are making and influencing our economic policy (both parties) are often either acting in their own economic or political self-interest, are fools, or just plain wrong. The course they have plotted can only end in fiscal chaos, and this book is an effort to chronicle these momentous events in advance. I want it to stand as a monument of protection against this happening again in my children's or my grandchildren's lifetime. That's how sure I am that I'm right.

I'VE BEEN THERE

When I wrote the first edition of this book in 1977, I felt that I was at an awkward age: too old to be useful, and too young to be an antique. Such introspection has come with increasing frequency as I have seen my youth fading, my time growing shorter, and my uncompleted agenda getting bigger. But as I reflect back over a long life that, by anyone's standards, would have to be called unusual, I believe that the big reason for my success over the years is simple: No matter where my readers are, I've either been there, or am just about to arrive.

There is hardly anyone out there in reader land that I can't identify with in some way. I've held on to *Ruff Times* subscribers over the years through good times and bad, even through two years when every investment market in the world was declining, making it next to impossible to be a hero. I think it's because I can identify in some way with almost all of you.

Young couples? Our last baby (#9), Terri Lynn, was born when I was fifty-two. She made me feel young all over again. I can identify with your feelings—the miracle-a-minute unfolding of new life, the heart-stopping sensation when your precious little one chokes momentarily on too big a swallow of milk, the sickening feeling that the national debt will end up being dumped on your child's lap, the uncertainty over the possibility of nuclear holocaust. . . . I shared your fears and your delight in watching a new personality taking shape. I loved watching my wife glowing with warmth and pride as she poured her love into the newest member of the Ruff family.

Above all, I understand your fears for a volatile and uncertain future. I can identify!

Retired folks? I have no intention to retire until they cart me away from the business field of battle, dead, senile, or incapable of communicating. Given my good genes (I picked my ancestors very carefully), my obsession with nutrition, and above all, the loving, low-stress environment my family creates, you'll be hearing from me for at least five to ten more years. Nevertheless, I can understand, on the real gut level, those of my generation and those who got there ahead of me as they contemplate the uncertainties of falling earning power and rising, inflation-driven expenses. I can identify!

Up to your ears in debt? Broke? Here, I can really identify. I grew up broke. We were too poor to afford a father. I know what it's like to not have things the other kids took for granted. I saw what a sacrifice it was for my mother to see that I got a dime for mowing the lawn every week so I could go to the Saturday matinee. I know what it is like to not have a car in the family, to be the only one left in our neighborhood without a TV set, to never own a home, but to always live in rented second- and third-story walk-ups. And then I know what it's like to have made it big, and suddenly lose it.

Everything with which I identified my ego and my success was ripped out from under me in 1968 when I failed in business. I had a wife and five children at the time, and the bittersweet memories of a beautiful boy killed in a drowning accident just a few months earlier. I will never forget the grinding struggle with myself to reestablish my confidence and find the appropriate vehicle to carry me back on top of the world so I could pay off a half million dollars in debts from which I had been legally discharged, but which I had made a solemn vow to my wife and to God, would be repaid someday.

When you tell me your financial troubles, don't expect me to feel sorry for you. You've never lost until you've surrendered. If you took everything from me today, in two years I'd be better off than I am now, because I now know that making money in investment markets or a business or profession is purely and simply a matter of attitude and hard work. If you believe you will achieve, you will. That overworked, oversimplistic-sounding platitude is the heart and soul of success. I can identify!

Are you rich, or at least prosperous, and worried about losing what you've worked so hard for? I can identify. I've been well-off twice, as I am now, so I understand the frustration of having to take valuable time away from work, family, or fun to cope with the mind-boggling complexities of trying to protect what you have from inflation, the IRS, or markets that continually probe for your character weaknesses so they can rip away from you the fruits of your labors.

I understand the resentment you feel over those who never

worked, risked capital, or beat their heads against stone walls to acquire wealth, who vote for the government to play Robin Hood and take it away from you and give it to them. I can identify!

A single parent? I've never been one, but my mother was. I have immense respect for those courageous men and women who manage to be effective parents and breadwinners. I saw the tears of frustration in my mother's eyes when she could not give me what she thought I should have. Many a time I saw her on her knees, seeking counsel and guidance from the Heavenly Father she trusted so deeply. I can identify!

Live in a big city? I grew up in one. I watched perverse social doctrines turn Berkeley and Oakland, which were once beautiful residential cities with all of the old-fashioned values, into hotbeds of revolution, envy, and strange economic theories. Not just coincidentally, they have become dependent on government and resentful of achievers. They have powerful political constituencies who, motivated by envy, want to destroy everything I have worked hard to earn. If they can't have it, they don't want me to have it, either. I can identify!

Live in a small town? Are you a farmer? I can identify. I used to live in a little farm community of 1,700 people, and I went fishing, to church, and to little league games with people who have grown up in small towns, who come from generations of farmers and fine, solid, salt-of-the-earth families who are the backbone of America, whose forebears pioneered the wilderness and created real wealth.

I've also seen the demoralizing effects of farm subsidies and regulations. I see the character worn into weathered faces and the wise eyes surrounded by wrinkles caused by years of squinting into the sun while riding a tractor or clearing ditches. These are good, wise people who often amaze and shame me with their instinctive sophistication in financial matters. I no longer underestimate them. I can identify!

A grandparent? Kay and I have 69 grandchildren, 55 of whom are within forty-five minutes of our home, and who like to come to our house to see us and our dog, Sugar—or maybe they come to see Sugar, and we just happen to be there.

I've been a small investor and a big investor. I've won big and lost big in the markets. I've made every stupid, costly mistake there is, and usually told my subscribers about it in a column called Ruff Gooffs so they can learn to avoid the same pitfalls. I've succeeded in business and failed. I've been depressed and euphoric. I've loaned and borrowed. I've been there, and I care.

Over the years, I've learned that deductive and inductive reasoning, as valued as they may be, sometimes have to yield to intuition in the investment markets. I spend hours each day reading, and I read fast. I process mountains of data, and I forget very little of what I've read, if it is interesting to me when I read it, and the range of things that interests me is very broad. Though I can call on others for research to crank into my internal databanks, there comes a time every several months when the indicators are mixed and contradictory. Then I have to turn to my dependable resource, a very deep and very wise computer-like level of the subconscious. Out of this deep well comes "hunches," "inspirations" . . . sudden flashes of insight, and an insistent voice that sometimes tells me, "Ignore the data in front of your eyes. I've added it up for you, and it's not what you think."

Now is when that intuition, drawing on the years of emotional and intellectual experiences, and stored data from digesting hundreds of millions of words, and the sheer gut instincts that come from living with the markets like a remora attached to a shark, will have to be trusted. We are at a most important market fulcrum.

MY POINT OF VIEW

I never have professed to be infallible, even though my track record says I'm right more often than I'm wrong. But I must try to protect you against my fallibility by giving you advice that won't hurt you, and alternative plans in case I am wrong or if my timetable is off. I must help you limit your risk. The investment marketplace is always rational in the long run, but it can be downright schizoid on any given day—and is often totally logic-proof for weeks or months at a time. Just remember, small losses caused by being a bit early or a bit late on your investments should be written off as premiums paid for an insurance policy against the worst case, just as all automobile insurance policies are mentally written off as protection against the crash you fully expect *not* to have.

Everything I am advising you to do, I have done myself, within the limits of my financial resources, as I am comfortably well off. Those who will gain the most benefit from this book are those who have some savings or some assets, small or large, such as equity in a home. You can benefit even if your resources are quite limited. You can start your personal and financial survival program with as little as fifty dollars a month for a few months. Everyone can do something, if it's only to vote out of office those fools who keep digging our hole deeper.

Throughout this book you will find references to books, publications, services, and products along with some candid "consumer's guide"–type comments. To assist you in your search for them, I have listed all of these in Appendix A, giving addresses, e-mail addresses, and phone numbers. Each product or service so listed, when referred to in the text, will be referred to this appendix.

I will make commercial recommendations, but I want to establish that I'll receive no financial rewards from those recommendations. I only sell my own advice—but none of the investments or products discussed in this book, and my other books, which are generally available on my website (www. rufftimes2.com), and, of course, *The Ruff Times*. If exceptions develop, I will disclose them up front.

In some instances, both my interest and my expertise in some of these commercial areas arose out of my past involvement in similar businesses. For example, out of my zeal for such products, I got into the food storage and supplement business in 1972 and designed one of the food storage programs I described and recommend in part II of edition I. I sold that business in November 1975 specifically to avoid the understandable confusion on the part of the media regarding my motives and so my recommendations would be fully credible.

If I had not been in the trenches in that business, I would not have had the experience necessary to be a competent adviser, nor understood the various ways you can make serious mistakes. In each case, when I do recommend a firm and a product, I try to negotiate the best deal I can for those who solicit my advice, consistent with maintaining the financial health of the recommended business.

These firms I mention are all dependable and have been around for years. They are not the only good firms in existence, but I prefer to find a few good solid companies in each area, negotiate a good deal for you, and monitor them closely to see that they conduct their business honorably and conservatively. Refusing all commissions has cost me a lot of money in the short term, but I believe it has been a big factor in helping to make my newsletter the most successful one in the country over the years. Better than that, I enjoy the love and respect of my children, who know that their father passed up money for principle.

Coming Attractions

Now a word about what to expect from this book.

In Part I, I describe the problems we face, then present the case for my economic theory. You will learn why more and more people are beginning to realize that the traditional "widows and orphans investments" such as blue chips, utility stocks, bonds, most mutual funds, CDs, cash-value insurance, and even your IRA and 401 K are crummy investments for now. Some investments that would have been considered the riskiest in past years will now be the safest in this difficult world.

Part II deals with the basic strategy for "personal survival" through the most difficult early stages of a confused and disrupted marketplace.

Part III will tell you how to hold your own financially and preserve the purchasing power of your investment assets. You win the inflation game if you break even in purchasing power, after taxes and expenses, but I think you can do much better than that. It's a low-risk, low-management-time strategy for maintaining and growing your purchasing power through the inflation period in order to take advantage of bargains at deflated prices later.

If you have the right attitude and have kept your purchasing power intact by following the strategies we'll discuss later, you can become more than wealthy, reaping many hundreds of percent return, as you catch the three basic changes in direction—the inflationary takeoff, the downward break, and the point when the recovery begins, or reasonably close to it. Exact precision in timing isn't necessary.

Now . . . it's time for Ruffonomics 101 to begin.

How to Prosper During the Coming Bad Years in the 21st Century

PART 1

RUFFONOMICS 101

I have written from the point of view of an "economic ecologist." Ecology is the study of the interrelationships of living organisms and their environment. The economy is also an "ecology." Most economists study only numbers and put them into computers and let the computer tell them what the world will be like. That can lead to false conclusions, because it excludes the human equation. Economic forecasting is as much an art as it is a science. If we do not study the whole "ecology"—man's religion and ethics, his moral behavior, government regulation, and politics as well as laws, money, and fundamental economics, we will not understand the economic environment and we will make lousy decisions with our own money. For that reason, my scope will be broader than you might have thought in a book that purports to give financial advice, but I think you will be surprised when you find out how much impact human moral behavior has on the economy, your taxes, and the world in which you live.

When I attended BYU, I was planning on a musical career,

so I majored in Music Education, but I picked a minor out of thin air: economics. I found the classes fascinating and it triggered my interest in the subject, but to my chagrin, as I became more sophisticated and my knowledge evolved, I found out that most of what I had learned in my economics classes was not true. I say that with some reluctance because I'm a fan of BYU and loved my university experience, but it is true. The Economics Department was not much different than in any other university, based on Keynesian economics, which has influenced governments and has since been mostly discredited, although a few elements of it are still true.

In developing my economic philosophy, I relied heavily on the works of Ludwig von Mises, Friedrich Hayek, and others of the Austrian school of economics. I became good friends with Hans Sennholz, an economist of the Austrian school, who taught me much and influenced my philosophy. These fundamentals give us a far better description of how the world works and how it will react to different influences. The Chicago School of Economics produced a distinguished graduate, Milton Friedman, who developed "monetarism," which is close to the Austrian school.

Because Ruffonomics provides the best explanation of why things work as they do and a much firmer basis for forecasting, I have added this section to this edition so you can understand where I am coming from, and perhaps change your philosophy from the prevailing economics. I promise not to go down deep and come up dry.

1

THE WATERSHED
YEARS

Much of American wealth is an illusion that is being secretly gnawed away, and much of it may be completely wiped out in the future.

The American experiment is, without a doubt, the most incredible social and economic phenomenon of all time. Everywhere I travel in America, I see evidence of great wealth: hundreds of thousands of beautiful residences and vacation homes, millions of boats, airplanes, and expensive cars, roads jammed with motor homes, expensive restaurants with people standing in line for hours for the privilege of spending a lot of money, and casinos in Las Vegas and Atlantic City jammed with wall-to-wall gamblers. Nothing in man's history has ever come close to it, and yet the forces are already irresistibly in motion to assault much of it.

Have you ever played "the neighbor game"? Your spouse says to you, "Dear, I wonder how much money Jones next door makes?" You consider the new boat, the Mercedes in the driveway, and the European vacation, and you say, "Well, he probably makes $250,000 a year." But you didn't estimate Jones's earnings, you only estimated what Jones spends, and the odds are that the Joneses are spending much more than they make, and they can only do so as long as someone will loan them the difference. And the day may not be far away when a lot of Joneses, all caught in the same whirlpool of debt, won't be able to make their payments. And most of the Joneses and their creditors will be wiped out.

Everything Jones has is "on the cuff"—mortgaged to the hilt. Debt is as American as apple pie, to say nothing of hot dogs and Chevrolet. We got here by borrowing and spending. The Joneses did it, your city does it, your state does it, and Uncle Sam does it. Oh boy, does he do it. Does Uncle Sam spend like a drunken sailor? No way! A drunken sailor spends his own money. We got here by spending money that isn't ours, created out of nothing, and while our ability to spend went up with our debt, the value of our assets is daily being ripped away as the inevitable result of our borrowing and spending—*inflation*. And this is the monster that will devour us.

But It Doesn't Have to Happen to You!

I will try to persuade you that America is racing toward its greatest test since the Civil War—the rising price of oil and gas from unstable and often hostile sources, and a monetary inflationary spiral leading to a depression that will be remembered with a shudder for generations, and whoever is elected president of the United States in 2008 and presides over the collapse will be "the Hoover of the 2000s," and the opposing party will win against his party for the next fifty years. There's a better-than-even chance that we will be well into it even before the next election, in which case the next president will be elected president of the *Titanic*. And if he or she should escape it, it will get his or her successor for sure.

No one knows exactly where the breaking point is, but it's coming. As you read this edition of this book, America is truly on the brink, and so is the rest of the world, because when America sneezes the rest of the world gets pneumonia.

So what is likely in your future? A grisly list of unpleasant events—exploding inflation, probable price controls, shrinking of the purchasing power of your savings (possibly to nothing), soaring gas and oil prices, imploding home equities, a collapse of private as well as government pension programs (including Social Security), vastly more government regulation to control your life, the disintegration of the basic foundation of society— the traditional family—and eventually an international monetary holocaust that will sweep *all* paper currencies (especially the dollar) down the drain and turn the world upside down. Paper fortunes based on lending will implode, and a new kind of investment and financial planning morality will put some very unlikely people at the top of the heap. And you can join them there, if you know what to do before the heap turns over.

You don't have to be a genius if you can identify the basic trends and make some very simple decisions with your assets. You might be too early, but that's okay. Do it now, and wait. You'll be vindicated. And I'd rather be a year or two too early than a week or two too late.

Here is the most likely scenario:

In the next recession (residential real estate is collapsing as I write), which will happen sometime after the publication of this book, deflation, recession, and unemployment will threaten the public welfare. Washington will react in its usual panic fashion to attack the problem by cranking up the spending machine to "stimulate" the economy—"a bit of the hair of the dog that bit us." Job programs, matching funds, universal health care, guarantees, subsidies, loans, and social spending programs will be triggered by events, such as the need to replenish state unemployment funds (most state unemployment funds will be broke even before the recession starts) and underfunded private pensions, and keeping major businesses from going bankrupt, to say nothing of banks, and bailing out broke cities and states. This will create a flood of newly created dollars, which is the engine of inflation. You will see a gradual accelerating inflationary spiral, probably followed by another government panic move—price controls.

Price controls will fail to stem the inflationary tide; they always do. These distortions in the economy, and the flood of dollars coming from "the printing press," to cover more than $50 trillion of unfunded liabilities, will cause Americans to distrust their own paper money and start to get rid of it as fast as they can in an orgy of spending, similar to what happened in Argentina when their inflation was running at 800% a year and Argentinians were buying everything in sight as inflation hedges.

When Kay and I were in Brazil, they were suffering from 800% or more inflation. We tried to go to a recommended curio store, but it was closed for two days. When the owner finally showed up, he told us why he had been closed for those two days. He explained, "Inflation is driving up the price of my wares so fast, I can't afford to sell them."

Sooner or later, the American dollar will no longer be a dependable means of exchange (it is already no longer a store of value), creating chaos in the marketplace. In the final stages, the government will probably make one or two abortive attempts to issue a new currency by "fiat" (official order), and this "fiat" currency will be rejected because of lack of trust. All currencies depend on confidence. After all else fails, the government will finally be driven by desperation to reestablish a gold-backed currency, but because it has already sold much of its gold hoard, gold will have to be revalued upward to a price adequate to back the new money—perhaps thousands of dollars per ounce (the international free market will have already done that). This will be the only way to establish a means of exchange and a store of value that people can trust.

A tiny minority who have no need for a means of exchange during this chaotic period (who have already bought several months' supply of all the things they will need, such as food, clothing, candles, medicine, toilet paper, batteries, diapers, soap, automobile parts, etc.; see chapter 7) will get along fine. Those who have no acceptable means of exchange or store of value, and no advance storage program, will suffer. But eventually (we hope) order will be reestablished, and painfully the nation will climb back out of its pit, hopefully chastened and prepared to avoid the mistakes of the past 50 to 100 years, but "net-lenders" will have been wiped out and paper fortunes will have disappeared.

If you're still with me after this rather scary prognosis, I will tell you: 1) how we came to this brink; 2) why this is the most likely scenario; and 3) what you can do to get through it, and even get wealthy. I will unfold the plan piece by piece in part III, after I've depressed you in part I. Then I'll summarize it for you in the last chapter.

This is no "bail-out-of-civilization-and-head-for-a-retreatin-the-Rockies-with-a-machine-gun-turret-on-the-roof" plan. And this program is not just for the rich. There are obviously some things that you can't do if you don't have enough money, but the basics will substantially raise your odds of personal and financial survival and can be implemented by nearly every middle-class family.

So the program is simple in concept:

1. Identify the trends, the pitfalls, and the opportunities in advance.

2. Survive the ensuing difficulties in good health.

3. Make the right moves ahead of time that will preserve and enhance your purchasing power, and that's not as hard as it may seem. I will give you a total strategy, a plan that should get you through to the other side in enhanced financial condition.

I repeat: I am not forecasting the end of the world, the end of Western civilization, or even the end of the American dream. America has survived a Civil War, at least three total monetary collapses, and several depressions. The inherent strength of the American system is incredible. It is the Rasputin of world economies.

Rasputin, "the mad monk," was a Russian Orthodox priest who achieved great influence over the czarina of Russia just prior to the Bolshevik revolution. Many believed he was a holy man, capable of great miracles. He was certainly capable of prodigious excesses of appetites, including legendary sexual feats. Eventually a palace conspiracy decided to murder him. (I've been on the spot at the restored palace where he was murdered, which is now a museum in St. Petersburg,

Russia. With the curator as a guide, we walked through the murderous events.) First, they fed him huge drafts of poison that would have killed ten lesser men and he didn't even belch. Finally, he was stabbed, shot, and had his skull fractured with a candelabra, and still he wouldn't die. They then dumped him through the ice in the Neva River and he clambered back onto the ice, terrifying his would-be assassins.

The American economy is the Rasputin of the 2000s. For 230 years it has endured incredible insults and fended them off with marvelous resilience. Despite the inflationary excesses of government and the creeping bonds of tyranny from government agencies, it is still the marvel of the world. My guess is that nothing can really kill it, although it will get terribly sick, but somehow, someday, it will come staggering back, like Rasputin, as it did from the depths of the 1930s Depression.

Does this sound like the end of the world as we know it? I don't know how to prepare you for the end of the world, so I'm not even going to try. If that happens, about all you can do in that exigency is be spiritually ready for anything that comes, and that's a matter between you and God; however, I think we should simply prepare prudently for the worst possible case for which practical preparations are possible.

I'm not against anyone doing anything with which he feels comfortable, as long as "he doesn't do it in the street and scare the horses," as Lady Astor said. I will just assume that America can come staggering back. In the meantime, I will save and wisely invest as much money as I can so my family can be as comfortable as possible through these difficult times and be prepared to take advantage of the investment opportunities that will inevitably arise.

This can be a time of great opportunity, and more opportunities will come as it plays out. My message is one of realism and hope in roughly equal doses, coupled with The Plan.

I do not write "for the edification of great experts," but for the "little guy" (or the "big guy," for that matter) who wants to make it safely from here to there and doesn't care how elegantly the theory is presented. There is a minimum of jargon and difficult-to-understand concepts. My goal is to make this program so understandable that everyone in your family will be able to understand this strategy.

Between now and 2010 is a watershed period. Great fortunes are made when rapid economic changes occur, in either direction. Although everyone likes the steady upturns, greater opportunities to make money can be grasped by those who catch the more violent swings and know what to do, even if it's only to avoid the fate of the unaware, who can be wiped out.

I am frequently challenged by the question, "Rather than telling individuals to prepare for possible bad times, why don't you devote the same energy and influence to changing things—to turning things around and preventing these problems?" The answer is that some trends are irreversibly beyond the point of no return, and by the time you've finished this book, you'll understand why. The juggernaut is headed for the precipice, and it doesn't matter whether we go soaring over the cliff with our foot on the accelerator (inflation), or skidding with our foot on the brake (deflation).

The world is best served by those who act in their own self-interest to protect themselves and their families, with due regard to basic principles of honesty, ethics, and morality, and the other guy's personal and property rights. For example, if and when the time comes when food is short, due to hitches in the distribution system due to soaring fuel costs, which

I believe is likely, the people who have stored food in advance will not be competing for scarce goods, and there will be more for everyone else.

I am reminded of the story of the little girl who whined, "I can't think of anything to do." Her mother found a map of the world in a magazine and cut it out along the lines of each country into a big jigsaw puzzle. She told Mary to put it all together, thinking it would keep her busy for hours. Minutes later Mary came back whining, "I still don't have anything to do." Her mother checked to see if Mary really was through with the puzzle, and sure enough, she was. So Mother asked, "Mary, how did you do it so fast?" To which Mary responded, "There was a picture of a family on the other side. I put the family together and the world turned out just fine."

The moral in that story? If each traditional family will become solvent, self-sufficient, and panic-proof, the world is better off, and that's what this book is all about—becoming panic-proof.

What If I'm Wrong?

What if my more dire forecasts don't come true? What if, like in the early eighties, the nation has a sudden rush of brains to the head and inflation is brought under control? Hallelujah! I'll lead the cheering section. We'll all be better off. Inflation is now embedded deeply enough in our society now that it is already creating a bull market in gold and silver and most commodities. That's where my counsel is based. So we will simply make a lot of money and try to sell near the top, as I did in the 1980s. If the world suddenly and unexpectedly turns sane again, we will go back to recommending dollar-denominated investments as I did in the eighties and nineties.

The things I have suggested you store in chapter 8 will simply be used up in the normal course of life. It is like an insurance policy where you get to consume the premiums, rather than losing them forever, like life or car insurance premiums; no harm done. There is a real possibility that the events of the next few years could turn modest amounts of money into real wealth.

Decide what degree of difficulty you can accept, and proceed accordingly!

Most of you readers are not Wall Street investor–types. Many of you have never invested in your lives, and some have never thought seriously about the economic facts that influence the world around you and underpin my financial advice. And most of the stuff you hear from the gurus on the financial shows or investment books is crapola. Consequently, I decided to write this new edition so you can understand the fundamental economic reasoning that underpins my recommendations and forecasts.

Let's look at the truth as Ruff sees it, in many cases based on Austrian economics.

THE HISTORY OF THE GOLD STANDARD

History tells us that for centuries gold and silver coins were universal currencies. But when the printing press was invented, so was paper currency. The first mass-printed paper currencies were mere warehouse receipts for gold or silver in a storage facility (think "bank"). Over the years, it became obvious that it was easier to merely give the receipts to the seller than go to the warehouse with the receipts and get the gold and silver to effect a transaction. In effect, we were on "a gold standard," with "gold-backed paper." Paper has become currency in common usage, and over time the people began to think of the receipts (currency) as money all by itself.

Then, as governments began to buy votes or finance wars, they yielded to the temptation to simply print more "receipts" than there was gold and silver to back it up (who would know?), each time with more dilution of the currency, triggering more and more price inflation (less-valuable paper currency). The foundation was laid in America when Roosevelt created the New Deal, which required more currency to pay for all the new government programs. Then Lyndon Johnson financed the War on Poverty and the Vietnam War at the same time (guns and butter), and the printing presses have had to step up the pace ever since. The process of currency dilution and destruction has been accelerating, with advances punctuated by retreats, since the thirties. Throughout history, this has been the case over and over again ever since the birth of paper money. The critical moment in this era came when Nixon "closed the gold window" (not allowing foreigners to exchange their dollars for gold or silver at the Federal Reserve), finally accepting reality as he saw it, and permanently detaching the paper dollars from gold. He got away with it, and the public accepted it, and the money printers were off to the races.

They put the final nail in the coffin in 1965 by no longer making 90% silver coins.

In the last ten years the Fed has manufactured trillions of fiat dollars out of nothing at by far the fastest pace in history, and it's accelerating. The Fed has then loaned the new dollars into circulation, or given them to politicians to spend. Since then, Congress has been spending like crazy. The money expansion since the late eighties now dwarfs several times over the monetary explosion that led to that historic metals bull market in the seventies. Gold and silver have been soaring recently in response (gold from $252 to $900, and silver from $4 to $14.70). Why can I be so sure that gold and silver are your protection against a shrinking dollar? History! Whenever the currency loses value (inflation) or drops against other currencies for a prolonged period, gold and silver go up, because a sagging dollar is inflationary, increasing the cost of the foreign goods we buy.

It's hard for me to exaggerate or overstate what is happening. Economists call this monetary expansion process "inflation." It really should be called "dilution"—dilution of the money supply, and consequently its value. This inevitably sooner or later causes rising consumer prices, which laymen (and the media—and even Wall Street) will mistakenly call "inflation." Calling rising prices "inflation" is like calling falling trees "hurricanes," but sooner or later consumer prices respond.

When will the public catch on? This is a slowly accelerating fact of life, and gold and silver prices are the measurement of public awareness. Sooner or later, awareness becomes a critical mass, and the metals go through the stratosphere. But for now, we have all become boiling frogs. First they put us in cold water, and then they turn up the heat, which we gradually tolerate, as we are boiled a bit at a time, until eventually we are cooked. If they just threw us into boiling water, we would all be scrambling to get out before we died.

THE FALLING DOLLAR

One early-warning harbinger of inflation is the dilution of the dollar until it starts to lose exchange value against foreign currencies, and the dollar, with fits and starts, has been in a long-term bear market for several years. A falling dollar is inflationary, as it takes more and more dollars to buy the increasing amounts of foreign-produced goods we are now buying. Wal-Mart's soaring sales are a telling indicator, as they are China's biggest customer for cheap goods produced by cheap labor. Gold and oil are quoted in dollars, so up they go. And now the metals are rising, not just against the dollar, but against nearly all currencies as the metals grow in strength, with some dramatic retreats, which are only opportunities to buy more. The falling dollar explains the early strength of the metals, and there is a lot more to come, as we continue to flood the international money markets with dollars, and now we don't even have to print them. This is now the age of "cybermoney," when less than 5% of the dollars are minted or printed, but are only computer entries at banks. We don't even know how many dollars there are! The Fed has recently stopped publishing key money-supply numbers (M3) without explanation.

2

UNFUNDED LIABILITIES: THE DOOMSDAY MACHINE

Do you need an unarguable reason to bet on inflation? Here's a reason that trumps all others.

On March 20, 2007, a statement that deserves but did not get banner headlines was made by David M. Walker, the comptroller general of the United States, in a poorly attended House subcommittee hearing. He said that "The federal government's financial condition and fiscal outlook *are worse* than many may understand." In this political season, no one seems to even be interested in the real financial status of the United States.

But how does this grab you? The government's total reported liabilities, net social insurance commitments, and other expenses are now "over *$50 trillion*" (that's trillion with a "t"); representing approximately four times the nation's total output (GDP) in fiscal year 2006, up from about $20 trillion, or almost two times the GDP, in fiscal year 2000.

"These structural deficits, which are virtually certain given the design of our current programs and policies, will mean escalating and ultimately *unsustainable* deficits and debt levels. Based on various measures and using reasonable assumptions, the federal government's current fiscal policy is unsustainable. Continuing on this imprudent and unsustainable path will gradually erode, if not suddenly damage, our economy, our standard of living, and ultimately our *domestic tranquility* and *national security*" (italics added).

If you think that's scary, you ought to read the entire report. What's really disturbing is that this congressional hearing, where the truth was boldly told, was poorly attended by members of the committee. They just weren't interested!

The most recent report, issued by the Department of Treasury on December 15, 2006, is available in full through the GAO (Government Accountability Office) at http://www.gao.gov/financial/fy2006financialreport.html, and at Treasury's Internet site http://www.fms.treas.gov/fr/06frusg/06frusg.pdf.

Walker elaborates, "One way to think about it is: If we wanted to put aside today enough to cover these promises, it would take about *$440,000* per American household, up from $190,000 in 2000. As these numbers indicate, the federal government faces large and growing structural deficits, primarily related to Medicare and other social insurance commitments. These structural deficits, which are virtually certain, will mean escalating and ultimately *unsustainable* deficits and debt levels" (italics added).

When Walker elaborated on the details, he told us that

"despite the reported increase in revenues in fiscal year 2006 ($255 billion), the federal government's costs exceeded its revenues by $450 billion. . . . As of September 30, 2006, the U.S. government reported that it owed directly (i.e., excluding unfunded liabilities) more than it owned (i.e., assets) by almost $9 trillion. In addition, the statement of social insurance in the financial report disclosed an additional $39 trillion of the government's social insurance responsibilities (unfunded), including Medicare, Medicaid, and Social Security. The total of reported liabilities, contingencies, social insurance, and other commitments and promises soared from $20 trillion in 2000, to about $50 trillion in the last six years.

Walker keeps repeating the real threats—Social Security, Medicare, and Medicaid—which represent "$39 trillion of the $50 trillion long-term fiscal exposure." Stated differently, "One would need approximately $39 trillion invested today to deliver on the currently promised benefits not covered by earmarked revenues for the next seventy-five years." Uncle Sam doesn't have the money. He spent it all to buy votes. Remember when we used to think a billion was a huge number? Multiple trillions are beyond comprehension. "Major reported long-term fiscal exposures in fiscal year 2006, with the present value totaling over $50 trillion, included about $1 trillion of other commitments and contingencies, and the $39 trillion of social-insurance responsibilities." He then reemphasized that this is up from $20 trillion in fiscal year 2000.

He kept coming back again and again to the cost of Social Security, Medicare, and Medicaid. Some years ago, early in his second term, Bush attempted to reform Social Security, based on the assumption that it was unsustainable. He was viciously assaulted politically by the Democrats and senior citizens' lobbying groups, like AARP, who assured us that there was "no problem" and that Bush was engaging in "scare tactics," and he was shot down in flames. Chapter 5 on Social Security tells the whole truth. Walker sums it up by saying, "Under either optimistic set of assumptions, the federal government's current fiscal policy is unsustainable."

I know this book will be attacked by the media, calling me a "prophet of doom," which, of course, is meant to make what I have to say politically incorrect. But, this is truth—the real hard truth. Unless these problems are courageously addressed and unless things change, the American dream will die a bitter, prolonged death.

If you are under forty, you had better plan your future without Medicare, Medicaid, and Social Security. Begin paying off your debts now so you can start earning compound interest on your savings, and invest in inflation hedges. When and if Congress faces this reality, they *won't* cut benefits, they *won't* increase FICA taxes, but they *will* inflate the currency. Your long-term future will be dictated by what you can scrape together and put into inflation hedges, starting now!

David Walker does not leave us without suggestions. He suggests that "closing the fiscal gap" would require spending cuts or tax increases equal to "eight percent of the entire economy each year over the next 75 years, or a total of about $61 trillion in present-value terms." To put this in perspective, "closing the gap would require an immediate and permanent increase in federal tax revenues of more than 40%, or an equivalent reduction of federal-program spending (i.e. in all spending except for interest on the debt held by the public, which cannot be directly controlled)."

He then goes on to say, "There is a need to engage in a fundamental review, reprioritization, and reengineering of the base of government. Allowing the government to meet the challenges and capitalize on the opportunities of the twenty-first century will require a fundamental review of what the government does, how it does it, and how it is financed. We need to address the growing costs of the major entitlement programs, and also review and examine all other major programs, policies, and activities on both the spending and the revenue side of the budget."

He also says, "The federal government needs to start making tough choices."

Walker recommends reengineering and reprioritizing all of the federal government's existing programs, policies, and activities, "to adjust to twenty-first-century challenges and capitalize on related opportunities." (I wonder what the related opportunities are.)

He then concludes, "As a result, the time to start is *now* to help save our future." It is amazing with such a pessimistic report that the man still retains his inherent optimism. I find that admirable, but I'm sorry, Mr. Walker, there is one basic problem, and that is that the government is growing so big it defies the ingenuity of human leadership. No one can grasp the totality of what the government does and how the government spends money. No one can do what's necessary without having everyone in America hate him (or her). Anyone who wants to be president of this mess must have something wrong with him or he needs a sudden rush of brains to the head. Ultimately, this dilemma will get us. We can only personally preserve our well-being and strength by protecting the American family, having our finances properly prioritized, getting rid of our personal debts, and starting to live for the future while no longer making promises we won't be able to keep.

In another interview, drawing parallels with the end of the Roman Empire, Mr. Walker warned there were "striking similarities" between America's current situation and "the factors that brought down Rome," including "declining moral values and (declining) political civility at home, an over-confident and over-extended military in foreign lands, and fiscal irresponsibility by the central government." Walker said, "In my view, it's time to learn from history and take steps to ensure the American Republic is the first to stand the test of time."

Mr. Walker's views carry weight, because he is a nonpartisan figure in charge of the Government Accountability Office, often described as the investigative arm of the U.S. Congress. He was appointed by Bill Clinton and is relentlessly apolitical. In an interview with the *Financial Times*, he said he had mentioned some of these issues before but now wanted to "turn up the volume." Some of them were too sensitive for others in government to "have their name associated with." "I'm trying to sound an alarm and issue a wake-up call," he said. "As comptroller general, I . . . take on issues that others may be hesitant, and in many cases may not be in a position to take on.

"One of the concerns is . . . we face major sustainability challenges that we are not taking seriously enough," said Mr. Walker. "With the looming retirement of baby boomers (8 million, 1/4 of the population), spiraling healthcare costs, plummeting savings rates, and increasing reliance on foreign lenders, we face unprecedented fiscal risks," said Mr. Walker. Current U.S. policy on education, energy, the environment, immigration, and Iraq also was on an "unsustainable path." "Our very prosperity is placing greater demands on our physical infrastructure. Billions of dollars will be needed to modernize everything from highways and airports to water and sewage systems. The recent bridge collapse in Minneapolis was a sobering wake-up call.

"They [the presidential candidates and the Congress] need to make fiscal responsibility and inter-generational equity one of their top priorities. If they do, I think we have a chance to turn this around, but if they don't, I think the risk of a serious crisis rises considerably."

We Owe It to Ourselves

As Dick Russell, editor of the *Dow Theory Forecasts* financial newsletter, says, "The country is mortgaged to the hilt. There is no unencumbered capital in America. The mountain of debt, public and private, including the federal debt, is much greater than the total wealth. The federal obligation alone is *twenty times more* than the total money supply. History records no example of any nation accumulating debt in anywhere near these relationships to the total national wealth, without eventually bringing down the entire economy and being liquidated, or repudiated, either through admitted bankruptcy, or the preferred form of bankruptcy—inflation. My guess is that we will liquidate our debt through the inflation process as the Germans did in 1923."

How can Uncle Sam accumulate such a mountain of contingent liabilities and yet get away with telling us that the national debt is only $650 billion? Well, it relates to accounting methods. The story is told of an Englishman, whose favorite hobby was ballooning, who decided to practice his favorite sport one Sunday afternoon. He miscalculated the wind and was blown across the English Channel and landed in a field somewhere in France. As he was lying there half stunned in the basket, a Frenchman rushed up. The Englishman said, "Where am I?" The Frenchman replied, "Why you are in a basket in the middle of a field." To which the Englishman asked, "Are you an accountant?" The Frenchman replied, "Yes I am, how did you know?"

"Because the information you have given me is completely accurate and totally useless."

One of the arguments that has always been used in favor of increasing the public debt is, "We owe it to ourselves," meaning that it is quite harmless.

Surprise! That is no longer true.

3

INFLATION: THE GREAT TRANSFER TAX

A modern Rip Van Winkle goes to sleep in 2007 and wakes up in 2017. His first thought is to find a pay phone and call his broker. He checks on his IBM stock, which was worth $25,000 when he went to sleep, and finds to his delight and amazement it is now worth $250,000. Just then the operator breaks in and says, "Your three minutes are up; please deposit a thousand dollars." That's what happens when inflation gets out of hand. And it will, because of the unfunded trillions of dollars worth of promises I described in chapter 2. To understand how that can happen, you must understand the nature of the inflationary beast, as it is the key to nearly every other problem in the future.

Inflation is *not* an increase in prices, although prices do increase. It is a *decrease* in the *value* of your money through oversupply and dilution. It means that every dollar buys less. This is not the first time it has happened. Inflation has brought down civilization after civilization. In the reign of Diocletian, around A.D. 300, the following letter was written by a Roman businessman to his agent in Gaul (France): "Hurry and spend all the currency you have. Buy me goods of any kind at whatever price you find them."

The value of money was dropping relentlessly and he wanted useful items, not cash, because the Roman Empire had been hit by such violent inflation that, to quote Emperor Diocletian, there were "increases in prices, not only year by year, but month by month, day by day, almost hour by hour and minute by minute." Rome unsuccessfully tried to solve its inflation by controlling, not merely prices, but the entire lives of most of its subjects, locking them forever into fixed places in the socioeconomic order. Rome attacked it, in short, by transforming itself into a totalitarian state, as rigid and all-pervasive as any the world has known. The Romans inflated the currency by mixing base metals with gold and silver in their coins, clipping them, and making them thinner or smaller, until everyone lost confidence in the money.

But that's old-fashioned now. We have the printing press. The brilliant economist Ludwig von Mises said, "Government is the only institution that can take a valuable commodity like paper, and make it worthless by applying ink."

The classic modern inflation, of course, is Germany in the 1920s, when they printed billion-mark notes on one side to save ink. You've all heard the story of the man who took a wheelbarrow full of money to the supermarket to buy a loaf of bread and he couldn't get the wheelbarrow through the door, so he left it on the sidewalk, assuming no one would steal the money because it was so worthless. He was right. When he came out, his money was scattered all over the sidewalk and the wheelbarrow was gone.

We had runaway inflation in China and in many parts of Europe after World War II. We've seen horrible inflation in Brazil, Peru, Argentina, and Chile, and we had an icy brush with the economic grim reaper here at home when the true U.S. true inflation rate hit around 18% in 1979, and England was grappling with 12 to 25% inflation. In each instance it has caused a decline in prestige and economic power, undesirable social changes, hardship, and more often than not, dictatorship. The Peruvian government had to declare martial law and battle rioters protesting 42% price inflation. Argentina once was a military dictatorship, with terrorist gangs shooting policemen and policemen organizing illegal vigilante groups and executing suspected terrorist sympathizers. When their inflation rate hit 800%, banks were offering 120% interest with no takers, and there, as well as in Chile, the temporary solution was to try to keep the lid on by repression.

The question that naturally arises is—why didn't the Argentine and Brazilian currencies finally collapse completely? They seem to have gotten inflation under control.

First, they are small economies existing in a world dominated by the dollar. They have the IMF, World Bank, and the great multinational banks to bail them out. Through dictatorship and international rescue operations, they apparently put a lid on their problems.

Second, their scenarios are not fully played out yet. When the U.S. inflationary monster escapes its cage, what will capture it? The IMF? The banks? When the world's dominant currency fades, everybody is in trouble, and no one is big enough to bail it out. Greece could fall in a Roman world without unsettling the world, but Rome couldn't.

The German inflation of 1920–23 created a fertile womb wherein a Hitler could be nurtured.

What is inflation? How do we get it, and what does it do to us? And will we see it bust loose here in uncontrolled form?

The term "inflation" means one thing to the economist and another to the public. Economists know that inflation is an increase in the money supply. We "inflate" the money supply by creating money, either through the printing press, through the fractional-reserve banking system, or the actions of the Federal Reserve, or a combination of all three. Only 5% of the dollars are minted, printed, or coined. The rest exists only in cyberspace.

When a country's money supply is fully redeemable in gold, there is built-in discipline as to how much money can be created. If a government knows it might lose its gold by redeeming too much paper money, the politicians should (in theory) be very careful how much money they spend and paper they print. As a result, it eventually becomes the objective of politicians in all paper-money economies to get rid of the gold standard and establish "fiat money" (unbacked money, declared to be money by government edict, or "fiat") so that more money can be created and more and more "benefits" can be "given" to its citizens to earn the gratitude of the voters. Alexander Tytler, a Scottish economist of the late eighteenth century, said that democracies fail when "the majority of the people discover they can vote themselves benefits from the public treasury." This is not likely as long as there is the discipline of gold-backing. Gold, that so-called "relic of barbarism," is maligned by the big spenders of today because it is their enemy.

Nixon "closed the gold window" at the Fed when it became apparent we had printed too much paper money, and foreigners were draining Fort Knox with redemption requests. Here's a simple analogy. If you went to an antique auction and you and everyone else in the room had $1,000 with which to bid, the highest price for which the antiques could be sold is $1,000. But if somehow you were able to put an extra $100 in cash or credit in the hands of some of the people in the room, the price of the antiques would go up, because there would be more money available to bid. The favored people who get the extra $100 would be the successful bidders and they would get the available goods. In the meantime, the purchasing power of all of the money in the room, stated in terms of antiques, would be less, as the price would "rise." The antiques had not changed, but the people's ability to buy them had decreased.

In effect, when any government creates money and spends it into existence by bestowing it upon its favored groups, their purchasing power is temporarily increased and yours is diminished, because this new money filtering into the free market auction place creates buying demand and bids up the price of everything. When your money cannot buy as much as it used to, the value of your money has declined. That's inflation!

Monetary inflation is a thief. It robs you who do not have wage-escalator clauses in your union contracts or whose income is fixed. That $300-a-month annuity that looked so good twenty years ago now assures only a not-so-genteel poverty. However, even those of you who have cost-of-living escalator clauses in your contracts are raped by inflation (and government is the pervert that does it) simply because the value of your savings is chewed away faster than you can earn interest. Inflation transfers your purchasing power to government as surely as if the government had taken the dollars away from you and spent them. Inflation gets at your savings, your bonds, your stocks, and your checkbook balances. In short, any monetary assets denominated in paper dollars are stolen from you.

So inflation is truly a tax.

Government can create money by printing it and loaning or giving it to veterans, minority businessmen, and so on, or even foreign countries, like China, that will eventually spend it, deposit it, or "invest" it in U.S. government debt. We can increase the money supply through the Federal Reserve, by allowing the banks to keep a smaller percentage of cash deposits on hand while loaning larger amounts of newly created money. In fact, money has a tremendous multiplying effect through the banks. Here's how (oversimplified).

If you had $1,000 in the bank and I asked you how much money you had, you would say, "I have $1,000." The bank doesn't keep that money safe and untouched for you. It is paying you interest, so it has to earn some money with it. Under the present rules, it can lend $850 of it to someone else. If you ask the person to whom they loaned it how much money he has, he will say, "$850." You still claim you have $1,000, so your $1,000 has grown to $1,850 and no one has printed or coined anything. His $850 gets spent and ends up in other checking accounts, which the banks can also use as reserves against which they will loan additional funds—up to 85 cents on the dollar, and this continues until roughly only 5% of the money supply in this country is actually printed or coined, and the other phantom 95% is in cyberspace and consists of computer bookkeeping.

Many economists (among them Milton Friedman and Arthur Burns) say that the money supply should be expanded at the same rate as the expansion of goods and services, so these two factors will balance out and it would not be inflationary. That's theoretically very sound. However, in the real world, human nature being what it is, and politicians being what they are, government cannot resist the temptation to buy votes, and, with their encouragement, the citizens vote themselves benefits from the public treasury. The politicians are unwilling to take the heat of voting to directly tax you to pay for all of it, so they create budget deficits, and Uncle Sam creates the needed money through the Federal Reserve, and the money supply increases at a rate faster than the real wealth. The net effect is an increase in prices, or, more properly, a decrease in purchasing power of each dollar. The net result is that you have been taxed to pay for the deficit. The inflation tax is hidden and not understood, which makes it the favorite of government.

No politician likes to vote for a direct tax bill, because he can become the visible target of your anger. Look at the Jarvis-Gann property-tax-limitation initiative in California as well as similar movements in other states. It succeeded because it was aimed at the most visibly repugnant of taxes—the property tax. Unfortunately, Jarvis-Gann also hit the most responsive, efficient level of government, the local level. The property tax was an easy target, because it hits with such an immense impact. If there had been a withholding property tax, and no regular assessment notices to remind you of how bad it is, and it just nibbled away at you a little bit at a time, there probably would have been no property-tax revolt.

The inflation tax is like a ghost. You can't get a handle on it. The average person doesn't have the slightest idea who causes inflation, so government can blame big business and big labor when they respond to the government-created inflationary spiral by trying to keep their purchasing power or profits up to snuff. Wages rise, then prices are boosted to cover wages, and higher wages are demanded again to keep up with increased prices, and they play a game of leapfrog that no one can win because there's no finish line.

As Pogo said, "We have seen the enemy, and he is us." It is our fault for two reasons:

1) Our ignorance. Few of us understand the process, so we let them get away with it.

2) Even if we understood the process, we would still like our personal benefits because they give us money to spend we did not have before, especially if you are one of the favored groups upon which government bestows its generosity. And, because your increased income gives you more borrowing power, you can increase your debt and spend more. And then you are one of the Joneses, living on borrowed money and borrowed time, and you are not about to give back your benefits.

According to a 1976 study by the North American Newspaper Alliance, back then approximately 56 percent of the people in this country were receiving tax money and were largely dependent upon it.

Retirees and pensioners (including dependents)	35,300,000
Disabled and direct support (including dependents)	10,500,000
Public assistance and unemployed (including dependents)	26,073,000
Government workers and dependents	47,251,000
Active armed forces personnel and dependents	5,137,000
Total People	**124,261,000**

This figure does not include workers for government contractors (Lockheed, etc.), merchants and suppliers serving the Iraq War troops, government installations and military bases, and those who use government services (farmers, small businessmen, private pilots, schools, etc.), and a zillion others, including all those who are looking forward to collecting Social Security someday. And those are 1976 figures. More than 70% were estimated to be in the same category in 2005. Don't bet on a significant number of these people giving back the money. Government money is like a cancer that has spread through more than 70% of society. The odds are seven to three it's got you, too. See if this composite biography sounds like anyone you know:

A young man attended public school, rode the free school bus, and participated in the subsidized lunch program. He joined the Army, and then upon discharge retained his National Service Insurance. He then attended the State University, on the GI Bill.

Upon graduation, he married a working Public Health nurse and bought a farm with an FHA loan, and then obtained an RFC loan to go into business. A baby was born in the county hospital.

Later he put part of his land in the soil bank, and the payments helped pay for his farm and ranch. His father and mother lived on his ranch on their Social Security; REA lines supplied him with electricity. The government helped clear his land. The County Agent showed him how to terrace it, and then the state built him a fishpond and stocked it with fish.

Books from the public library were delivered to his door. He banked his money and a government agency insured it. His children attended public schools, rode free school buses, played in the public parks, and swam in the public pools.

He was a leader in obtaining the new Federal building (he must be a constituent of Senator Byrd from West Virginia), and went to Washington with a group to ask the government to build a great dam. He petitioned the government to give the local air base to the County.

Then one day, after hearing about the multi-trillion budget, he wrote his Congressman.

"I wish to protest these excessive governmental expenditures and attendant high taxes. I believe in rugged individualism. I think people should stand on their own two feet without expecting handouts. I am opposed to all socialistic trends and I demand a return to the principles of our Constitution and of States' Rights."

Author Unknown

Winners and Losers

Inflation, like any other game, has some who win and some who lose. Let's list the losers first.

1. People who lend money. This includes those who have deposits in the bank, cash value in their life insurance, own first and second mortgages, and bonds—corporate, municipal, or federal. It's very simple. They will be paid back in dollars of less value than the ones they loaned. If the inflation rate is 10% and you receive a 10% return on your investment, you are breaking even. Or are you? Let's go back and look at that again. If you paid 20% taxes on your interest, here's how it would work out.

	$1,000	invested (loaned)
+	$100	earned interest
	$1,100	total
Less	$ 20	income tax
	$1,080	
Less	$108	annual purchasing-power loss (10% inflation)
	$972	remaining value of your capital
	$28	net loss in purchasing power (2.8%)

A slight loss, right? But, if you depend upon the interest for your living expenses and you spend the $80 (your after-tax earnings) to live on, where do you stand?

	$1,000	invested (loaned)
+	$100	earned interest
	$1,100	total
Less	$20	income tax
	$1,080	
Less	$108	purchasing-power loss (10% inflation)
	$972	value of your capital
Less	$80	spent to live on
	$892	remaining value of your capital
	$108	net loss in purchasing power (10.8%)

You now have $108 less purchasing power than you started with—a loss of 10.8% per year.

So there you are, folks. You have been taught to only spend your interest, and never touch your capital. Right? Well, if you are spending your interest, you are consuming your capital.

How high a rate of return do you have to have to break even? In a 10% inflationary world, assuming a 20% income tax rate (unrealistically low, but I don't want to load the case to make my point), you need a return of almost 20% on your money to break even and earn a true 4% return, after taxes and inflation. Unless, of course, you reinvest all the interest proceeds, in which case you still need about a 15% rate of return to break even after taxes and inflation. And if your tax bracket is higher than 20%, it's even worse. Now, do you believe inflation rips off the lender?

2. **The saver is a loser** if he puts his money in a bank and earns a rate of return lower than the rate of inflation, because he's really a lender to the banker. If he buys a CD (certificate of deposit) to get a slightly higher rate, his money is tied up for a long period of time, and he can be destroyed quickly if inflation really gets going. Because spending beyond your means is basically immoral, and saving is basically moral and essential for the nation to be able to build capital for growth and investment, inflation forces us into lousy decisions, beginning with the conclusion that saving and lending is dumb, unless, of course, you don't understand the process and are dumb enough to continue to save and lend. Fortunately for the vote buyers and the bank's borrowers, the lenders and savers haven't yet caught on.

3. **Pensioners will lose big.** If you set up an annuity or are counting on your Social Security, your company retirement plan, your state or city pension plan, or your military pension, the purchasing power of those dollars will be worth only a fraction of their original value by the time you get them.

What about IRAs and 401K plans? They are based on the assumption that you can set aside tax-free money for retirement into an investment fund and have it earn for you tax-free. When you do take it out years from now, you will supposedly be in a lower tax bracket. With an IRA (for wage earners) you can set aside up to $5,000 of your wages tax-free each year.

If that is such a good deal, why don't I like it? First, I don't think it's a safe assumption that you will be in a lower tax bracket. Inflation is accelerating us all into higher tax brackets. The odds are you will be in an equal or higher bracket and the tax savings will be nonexistent. Also, rising inflation will chew up your capital faster than you earn interest, and you'll get back cheaper dollars than you put in.

These plans are inflexible. It's hard to include gold or silver coins or bullion. It is difficult, costly, or impossible to switch them from one kind of investment to another, and with the changing environment you need to be prepared to switch between inflation hedges and paper. If you do, the tax penalties can be severe. I am most concerned with the totally inflexible programs offered by insurance companies that are oriented in the direction of paper investments. You are a lender. Even if the insurance companies don't go broke, the money is going to go broke, and you will be locked in. You will have climbed into a leaky lifeboat.

Some 401K plans allow you to invest in gold and silver, and you can also invest in mining stocks and mining mutual funds, which make them more acceptable. Several companies can help you—Investment Rarities, International Collectors Associates and Kitco. I am not an expert on these plans. I'll just point out how they fit into the future as I see it. With inflation in your future, the typical IRA or 401K can be a guaranteed instrument of confiscation over the long haul. Eventually the government will repudiate all of its debt by paying you off in worthless dollars. However, those who receive government pensions are a very potent voting bloc, and they probably will have their benefits increased to keep pace with inflation for some time, but eventually that will bankrupt the pension system because that burden will fall back on the rest of the taxpayers, and they'll revolt.

Medicare and Social Security will deliver the coup de grace (the final blow) by burying us all in unfunded liabilities (future promises without the assets or income to pay for them), as explained in chapters 2 and 4. The total as of now (and rising) is $39 trillion.

The Winners

I spend five hours a day reading newsletters, economic reports, magazines, and newspapers, and I've concluded that most financial advisers don't understand money and none of them understand politics. We have to look at the winners, and the losers who think they are winners, in order to understand why inflation is going to continue, and here they are.

1. **The government.** And who is the biggest borrower of all? Uncle Sam of course, with the cities and states next in line. They know they will pay off their debt in dollars worth far less than the ones they borrowed. In an inflationary spiral, the one who gets the money first and spends it on the right productive assets will gain the greatest benefit, because he spends it before it filters, multiplies, and compounds through the economy, driving up prices. That's precisely what government does. This practice is also a calculated, deliberate policy to inflate at a "controlled rate." Inflation is a form of bankruptcy and repudiation of debt, so they try to do it a little at a time to avoid alarming anyone. When it gets out of hand, they will do like the German government did in 1923

when they paid off all those patriotic German bondholders to the pfennig with money that had a total purchasing power of one American penny. The government didn't go broke, the money went broke, and the people who bought those bonds (the lenders) got ripped off. Uncle Sam is following the same process. Don't expect him to cut his own throat by really cutting inflation. He benefits too greatly.

2. **Homeowners** who bought bigger houses (if they sold before the recent collapse) by obtaining bigger mortgages. The bigger the house, the bigger the inflation profits. As inflation increased the price level of their homes, they saw their equity growing and they felt rich, and if they cashed in at the right time and got off the debt pyramid, they truly are. They will pay back their mortgages with very cheap dollars. In fact, in a real runaway inflation, you might be able to pay off your mortgage with one week's or one month's salary.

This payoff concept is presented beautifully in Benjamin Stein's novel *On the Brink*, a story of a not unlikely future when a White House decision is made, once inflation gets out of hand, to deliberately accelerate it so that millions of Americans with mortgages and debts can pay them off with a few days' salary. The idea is political dynamite for a while, as there are more debtors than there are mortgage holders and landlords. At least, that is the way it is perceived. Everyone ignores the fact that the solvency of their banks, their pension funds, and their insurance companies are at stake, and in the economic ignorance of the American people, they enthusiastically jump on the idea.

3. **Productive borrowers.** Those borrowers who use the borrowed money productively and cautiously to invest in coun-

tercyclical investments or a successful business do just fine. They will pay off their loans with cheap dollars and build fortunes through leverage.

4. **Some investors.** Those who invest early in chaos inflation or disaster hedges do best of all, especially if they use leverage wisely. This includes gold, silver, mining stocks, antiques, collectible items—those things to which people instinctively turn when the value of paper money is diminishing in an attempt to beat the loss of purchasing power that inflation brings, and in fact, that inflation *is*.

5. **Some sellers.** Those who merchandise these items. Anyone in the antique, art, stamp, bullion coin, or food-storage business should do very well during the runaway inflationary spiral, especially if they sell their businesses near the peak.

6. **The break-even crowd.** Anyone who gets through all this "even with the game" is a winner. He will have the resources to pick up some incredible bargains after the inflationary spiral has run its course and there's been an implosive collapse of the economy. There will be incredible bargains in stocks, bonds, real estate, and a myriad of other things, which we will discuss later, for those who had the foresight to preserve their purchasing power by buying inflation hedges.

Inflation is a genie that once let out of the bottle cannot be put back.

Inflation or Deflation?

In the seventies there was a great controversy among hard-money investment advisers (gold bugs) as to whether or not we are headed for more inflation or a destructive deflationary depression like in the 1930s. Remember the Maginot Line? When the Germans outflanked the Maginot Line with paratroops and fast-moving Panzer divisions, the guns were pointing in the wrong direction. Like the generals who built the Maginot Line, the deflationists are fighting the last war. Because the American decision-making generation is still re-living the last great deflationary depression of the thirties, our most predictable reaction will always be to inflate the currency to fight deflation and depression. We will not see serious deflation until a hyper-inflation has run its course. The people who propose that we will allow deflation simply do not understand politics or the human equation. Government will spend more than it collects in taxes and the Federal Reserve will accommodate their inflationary money requirements.

Let's examine why there will be no big deflationary depression until after inflation has devoured us.

Once inflation reaches a certain point, governments conclude, and quite rightly, that they must continue to inflate or die politically. If they do not inflate, their inaction will cause deflation (always a depression), and it will be obvious who caused it, and no politician wants his name associated with that.

The only way you can have deflation now is if the government deliberately stopped creating money at a rate needed to meet the demand for money, while voting to reward their constituents. Remember, deflation means an increase in the value of money. You can only increase its value if there is less of it. There will only be less of it if politicians and money managers suddenly get the guts to reverse the process and kick us into a deflationary depression as a deliberate act. That just ain't gonna happen, although they may try cautiously for a while until unemployment rises, business falls off, and the resulting political and economic pain triggers Uncle Feelgood into cranking up the money machine again.

Price inflation will develop a life of its own, independent of the monetary stimulus that will start it, because most everyone has a cost-of-living escalator built into his labor contract, and businessmen raise prices in anticipation of future price and wage inflation. Prices can even increase in the face of monetary contraction.

When price inflation reaches a certain point, it will cause disruptions in the economy that can only be solved with the Band-Aid of more money, and then only temporarily. For example, if you have 20 to 30% inflation, the whole American business and distribution system, which extends credit for 30 days, could periodically and randomly be interrupted. Take wheat, for example. The farmer sells grain to the elevator operator, who sells it to the miller, who sells it to the baker, who sells the bread to the distributor, who sells it to the supermarket chain, who accepts your check. At every point along the line, each link in the chain buys and sells on 30-day credit. If money is losing value at the rate of 20 to 30%, the party who extends 30-day credit has an inflationary loss on his accounts-receivable of 2 to 2.5% per month. Remember, those who extend credit get ripped off by inflation, so he either: 1) starts charging interest on what used to be net accounts (a cost that has to be passed on to the next level); 2) he demands cash, creating a new increase in the money supply to prevent interest rates from exploding out of sight; or 3) he just raises his prices. These price increases are compounded several times as they move through each step in the distribution chain until the effect at the retail price level is explosive. All three of these factors are inflationary, with a bias toward the printing press, and we can quickly move from a credit economy into a "printing press" economy.

It used to be that you could extinguish the inflationary fire by raising interest rates and taxes to reduce spendable income and cool off demand, while discouraging borrowing and expansion. However, our fire extinguishers are loaded with kerosene, as taxes and interest are merely passed on in the price structure to the next level. In fact, taxes help make inflation permanent.

There is no way a businessman can lower prices when so many of his costs are inelastic. During the Depression of the thirties, the businessman or manufacturer had only three primary cost factors to be concerned with—labor, materials, and distribution. When the prices of these things were falling, he could reduce retail prices, and he did. People didn't have much money, but you could buy a loaf of bread for a nickel then. Today, a businessman has inflexible and rising costs, including the costs of government regulation, property taxes, Social Security taxes, high interest rates, high wages protected by union contracts and minimum-wage laws, price-supported commodities, etc., and all these costs have to be passed on in his prices. Because of this, rather than reducing prices to stimulate demand when demand drops in a recession or depression, he plans to manufacture and sell fewer units and raises his prices to make more money per unit.

That's why during 1974 and 1975, when unemployment was high and the economy was coming to a screeching halt, we were heading for the highest rate of inflation the nation had seen in almost a century. So inflation is intractable, and don't let anyone "kid you otherwise." Unless, of course, government slashes spending, sells its printing presses, stops regulating, eliminates price supports and minimum-wage laws, and deliberately throws us into a gut-wrenching, election-blowing depression. Eisenhower held inflation to 1.4%—and lost both houses of Congress, and the Republicans didn't get them back for decades, so don't hold your breath.

Here's another possible scenario, explaining how we can become a "printing press" economy, or, in other words, how the government could be forced to start grinding out dollars.

Principle #1: The Germans went from a credit economy to a printing-press economy in a little over three years. Basically here's how it happened.

As government deficits and World War I reparations created demands for continuing increases in the money supply, interest rates began to rise along with the price-inflation rate. The rise in interest rates led to a fall in the value of bonds. Worsening economic conditions led to more demands on government, larger deficits, more inflation, and higher interest rates (as high as 10,000%), and eventually the bond markets collapsed entirely. The government, however, could not cut back on its spending because of the political demands of the people, so, rather than issuing bonds, which no one would buy anyway, they simply "monetized their debt," which means that, rather than going into the capital markets and borrowing the money to fund their deficits, they printed the money directly.

Principle #2: In our present economy, the government tries to fund its deficits by going into the capital markets and borrowing from the existing money supply, while maintaining a relatively steady growth in the money supply of around 4 to 5%. As the bailout demands on government increase during a recession, and the taxing system runs smack into a tax revolt, the deficits will begin to explode. Soon the government cannot meet its borrowing requirements from the capital markets without driving out all other borrowers and creating a horrendous depression, so they are forced to increase the cybermoney supply. But they can't increase it enough to ease the interest rate pressures. As interest rates continue to rise, bond prices collapse, (bond prices go down as interest rates go up) and it soon becomes too expensive (sky-high interest rates) or impossible for the government to borrow money, as people begin to thoroughly distrust any fixed-interest debt instruments (just as I and most of my subscribers do now).

The government then has an interesting choice: cut the budget, reduce spending, and cancel government programs, plunging us into a deflationary depression, and take the political flak, or go directly to the "printing press" and make more cybermoney. I am betting they will choose monetary inflation. There is no example in history of anyone having done otherwise, except military dictatorships, and fortunately, a military dictatorship would be hard to fully implement in this country. We don't have a national police force, and we don't have a big enough, dependable army to enforce it.

Principle #3: There are forces in motion that are increasing public demands on government sufficient to cause the deficit to explode in the next few years. As the dollar crashes, as it has been doing since 2000, foreign investors in U.S. government securities will bail out. If China, India, and Japan threaten to unload their trillions in U.S. Treasury paper, interest rates will be ratcheted up to make dollar-denominated investments more attractive. As we move into the recession, and cities and states find themselves in deeper trouble, it will require massive amounts of federal money to guarantee their bonds and provide the necessary unemployment insurance and other benefits. What will it be like when we get into an economic slowdown with rising unemployment?

If a worldwide depression strikes, the lesser-developed countries will default on their debt to the large banks, and Uncle Sam will have to trot out more dollars to bail out the banks. We are the lender of last resort for the entire world, due to the loans the big multinational banks have made to these countries, and the government will not allow those banks to go broke, even at the cost of hyperinflation. They *are* the monetary system of the world.

Cities, states, and the federal government in the next recession will be stuck with a problem of declining tax revenues and increasing demands on government to alleviate the suffering caused by recession, unemployment, and business slowdowns and to keep the blood out of the streets. While all of this is going on, this insane witches' brew of problems will be stewed in the pot of more inflation, as all of this printing press and cybermoney flooding the economy will result in high-velocity spending, with people frantically trying to keep up with the cost of living by buying before prices go up, but losing ground, and we will be faced with the spectre of inflation and depression at the same time. If you don't think that can happen, look at Germany in the early twenties. Look at the United States in 1974 through 1980. Think "stagflation." There are differences only in degree, not in kind.

Those who argue deflation are basically saying that paper money will increase in value, which means that would be the best holding of all. History records no instance of an inflationary spiral ending with a substantial increase in the value of paper money. And I wouldn't think it's about to happen now.

Will Rogers said, "Invest in inflation, it's the only thing that's going up." If you have to periodically buy something, and prices rise, you are hurt by inflation. If you already bought a lot of it when it was cheap, you are on good terms with the inflationary monster.

Parts II and III of this book will tell you how to do it. There are ways to ride to wealth through inflation, while limiting its damage.

4

SOCIAL SECURITY: THE PONZI CHAIN LETTER

Don't be alarmed by this chapter if you are currently getting a Social Security check or are over sixty. The big problems described herein will probably not occur until after you are gone, and it's too late to do anything about it, anyway. If, however, you or your children are under forty, worry a lot, and take this chapter very seriously.

Social Security, Medicare, and Medicaid are guarantees of an inflationary future. As this is written, they account for more than $39 trillion in unfunded liabilities (obligations supported by no income or assets) that can only be paid by inflating the currency (see chapter 2). Tens of millions of people don't question that Social Security will be there for them when they retire and will be enough for a comfortable life. Financial planners build this assumption into their clients' financial plans. For millions of Americans, this is a lie, and it is a very expensive and painful mistake to bet on.

Every time I express my politically incorrect views on this subject, I rub a lot of people the wrong way. Social Security is a sacred cow that we are not supposed to question. It is also called the "third rail of politics." When George Bush tried to reform it, the Democrats clobbered him by raising false fears, and the Republicans ran for the hills. But as the saying goes, "Fools rush in where angels fear to tread." I guess I'm a fool.

I may be beating a dead horse here; many of you already know in your heart of hearts that the FICA deduction from your paycheck is a big ripoff, but you hope that the day of reckoning will not come until after you have gotten yours. But if you are under forty, you may never see it, or it may be so inflation-ravaged that it won't buy much. It is by far the biggest Ponzi pyramid the mind of man has ever conceived, and, like all Ponzi schemes, it will see its day of reckoning.

Ponzi Revisited

Social Security is a perfect reflection of a classic fraud case of some years ago, when a man by the name of Ponzi raised funds from investors by promising huge payoffs as high as 40% a month. He did nothing productive with the money and earned no real profits for his suckers, but he paid huge "dividends" to attract previous investors *by using the money raised from new investors*!

The Ponzi pyramid eventually collapsed of its own weight, and Ponzi went to jail. It's considered a crime when private citizens do it, but it is considered "compassionate social engineering" when the government does it. As long as enough new suckers pay into Social Security to balance the books, the fraud holds up. But if the number of paying "marks" diminishes, due to a shrinking birth rate, until they cannot or will not balance the books, then the scheme collapses spectacularly.

Just understanding this truth may give you more incentive to begin preparing for a retirement that does *not* depend on Social Security—even if it somehow hangs together until you die. You can be far better off when you retire than if you just keep betting on Social Security as it is now constituted. You will also learn here why Congress will *never* fix it before it is too late to save it.

Most Americans believe that Social Security is supposed to take care of them in their old age, and they plan their lives accordingly, but it wasn't even intended for that in the beginning. It was only to be an income supplement to your personal savings and other pensions. Under *the most optimistic* scenario, Social Security alone wouldn't allow you anything but *genteel poverty* when you can no longer earn a living. Here are some hard truths:

In the most likely scenario, either Social Security won't even be there when you need it, or the money they will have to print to pay you your monthly check will cause a saber-toothed inflation that will so diminish the purchasing power of the money that it will be sliding toward worthlessness; so here are the rules to help you avoid a monumentally stupid mistake:

Rule #1: If you are under age forty, plan your future without Social Security. If you are over age forty, plan on seeing progressive benefit cuts, steadily increasing FICA deductions from your paycheck, and a growing inflation that shrinks the value of your benefits *when* —and *if*—you actually get them.

Rule #2: Don't retire at age sixty-five unless you are physically, mentally, or emotionally unable to be productive. Maintain your income stream as long as possible.

Rule #3: Accept personal responsibility for your own retirement income by becoming frugal and starting *now* to build a nest egg big enough to live comfortably on the interest *without* Social Security.

Let me explain the Social Security scam.

The following exchange took place thirty-two years ago during Senate Social Security hearings between Senator William Proxmire and a Mr. Cardwell of the Social Security Administration.

PROXMIRE: "There are 37 million people, is that right, who get Social Security benefits?"

CARDWELL: "Today between 32 million and 34 million."

PROXMIRE: "I'm a little high; 32 to 34 million people. Almost all of them or many of them are voters. In my state, I figure there are 600,000 voters that receive Social Security. Can you imagine a senator or congressman under those circumstances saying we are going to repudiate that high a proportion of the electorate? No.

"Further, we have the capacity under the Constitution, the Congress does, 'to coin money' as well as to regulate the value thereof. Therefore, we have the power to provide that money, and we are going to do it. IT MAY NOT BE WORTH ANYTHING WHEN THE RECIPIENT GETS IT, BUT HE IS GOING TO GET HIS BENEFITS PAID."

CARDWELL: "I tend to agree!" (emphasis mine).

Just to bring you up to date, 49 million people received Social Security benefits in the year 2000, twenty-five years later. The first big wave of retired baby boomers has started receiving retirement benefits in 2007 and 2008.

Social Security is the most dishonest, reprehensible, deceitfully unsound scheme ever foisted by the government upon a trusting public—a fraud so huge that the imagination is unable to grasp it, and they have made us willing accomplices to the fraud for 75 years. (Someday I will tell you what I *really* think!)

Try this short true/false quiz:

T   F   Payroll deductions for Social Security go directly into the Social Security trust fund "lockbox" where they are saved for your retirement.

T   F   Money deducted from *your* paycheck will be used to pay *your* retirement benefits.

If you marked both of these true, you score 0%. *All* your basic assumptions about the Social Security Trust Fund are probably false.

The national economy has become dependent upon the Social Security system. It disburses more funds than any other governmental subdivision. FICA is the biggest single tax paid by most Americans. The impact of changes in Social Security payroll taxes or benefits is immense, and if we increase or decrease either, the effects on the economy are complex and ultimately negative.

Pensioners are trapped in the system. Many are totally dependent upon it. According to the Social Security Administration, their Social Security check represents more than *half the income* of 64% of the recipients. Millions of people would be in for genuine suffering if the Social Security system were to go broke, or if benefits were to be cut, or if they were not increased to accommodate increased "cost of living." Even worse, though, is the easily demonstrable fact that rather than saving for their retirement—a good, old-fashioned, time-honored American tradition—millions have spent everything they earned, usually on debt payments, and have a touching level of faith in Uncle Sam to take care of them.

I have a tough question for you: What would your life be like if you were forced to retire at age sixty-five, and you were heavily in debt, and your principal income was your Social Security check? Well, I am about to make a big dent in this faith in a beneficent uncle in Washington with the truth—the unpleasant, unvarnished truth. You are about to learn why you must not make your retirement totally dependent on government retirement promises.

THE LOCKBOX MYTH: A GRIM FAIRY TALE

Let's reexamine your true/false quiz: "Payroll deductions for Social Security go directly into a Social Security Trust Fund 'lockbox' where they are saved for your retirement." During the 2000 presidential election, Al Gore made a big deal of the lockbox into which he would put your Social Security Trust Fund. It was a crock! If that's a crock, what is the truth?

When the government forces your employer to deduct Social Security taxes from your paycheck, *all* of this money, along with your employer's "contribution," goes into the General Fund. It is all used for current government expenses, and current Social Security checks are just a part of it. It is *not* held separate from other funds. The Treasury borrows *all* of it by issuing illiquid, nonnegotiable IOUs to the Social Security Trust Fund, and they constitute the whole fund—just under $1 trillion as of December 31, 2000. The Trust Fund has never seen any of that money, only these pieces of paper which represent that the government has taken the money and spent it, and will print more if necessary. All there is in the Trust Fund "lockbox" is a mountain of nonnegotiable government IOUs! The government uses a rhetorical trick to make this palatable; they tell us that "in the interest of safety," the Social Security Trust fund is "invested" in the safest possible instrument—U.S. Treasury securities.

These securities are a liability of the United States Treasury, secured by "the full faith and credit of the United States government," which means the printing press! When the fund disburses its monthly benefits, it merely calls upon the Treasury to issue checks. The government would do this even if there were no government IOUs in the fund. The cost to the taxpayer would be the same. It is just that everyone feels more secure if there are pieces of paper saying the government promises to do this. That's what makes the scam work and the public feel secure even as they are being robbed, but it really doesn't make any difference; the so-called Social Security Trust Fund is nothing more than a *glorified set of IOUs and bookkeeping entries!*

Just for form's sake, if they should issue more money than was collected for FICA, the Treasury merely retires some of those notes and the "Trust Fund" shrinks. If it issues *less* money than was paid out in current benefits, the Trust Fund is in "surplus," and the pile of IOUs grows.

How valuable is a Treasury security held by the Social Security system? If you were to write yourself an IOU, add it to your financial statement, and take it to the bank to obtain a loan, they would laugh you out of the bank. We cannot create real wealth by giving ourselves our own IOU. The Social Security Administration is a division of the United States government holding IOUs of another division of the United States government, which has spent all the money and has no assets of its own for collateral. This paper represents no value at all. It is not an asset, but an unsecured promise.

As a result, the political debate in the last election over whether the Social Security Trust Fund should be put in a "lockbox" is simply a deceptive discussion of cosmetics—the appearance of things. Already, current Social Security payments are paid from the General Fund. The so-called "depletion of the Trust Fund" or "dipping into the Trust Fund" is not the real threat to the system, nor is it new; it's the way it has always been. The real threat is the ever-rising tide of pension payments, supported by fewer and fewer workers.

There used to be 24 workers supporting each person in the system; now there are 2.5. Soon there will be less than 2. You are making a monstrous bet on your children's willingness to bear that increased burden, which in a few years will have to be more than 30% of their paycheck, until they won't dare take any more out of people's paychecks, lest it cause a war between the generations.

The Social Security system depends upon the younger people at the bottom of the pyramid believing that their payroll deductions will pay for their retirement, but that's not true, and it never was. The government plays games, and *we are conned*. Social Security payroll deductions are simply another method of raising money to fund the government's alleged "needs." Your FICA payroll deduction is a slush fund to pay for Defense, Agriculture, FTC, EPA, and the rest of the alphabet soup in Washington, as well as current Social Security benefits.

THE GOVERNMENT-CERTIFIED CHAIN LETTER

But the real fraud is the fact that the system is really a gigantic chain letter. Chain letters operate under the assumption that when you add your name to the bottom of the list and send your dollar to the name at the top, other suckers will add their name under yours so eventually your name will rise to the top and you will get money from the bottom. It pays off only if a continual new supply of workers continues to fall for it. Sooner or later, as the birth rate shrinks and the number of contributors shrinks and the number of recipients grows, it will sputter to a stop, and *the last guys in will lose out*.

Everyone *now* receiving Social Security will get payments until the day they die, so if you are a current recipient, you have nothing to worry about, but the real victims are those young workers who are paying into the system now through FICA deductions. They will pay rising and increasingly oner-ous FICA taxes, expecting to retire in 15, 20, 30, or 40 years. They will be ripped off when they retire, or they will be paid with inflationary funny money, which is another way to be ripped off.

The money taken from you is also used to pay benefits *to many who have paid nothing into the system*, as the system is being used to provide social benefits outside of the original intent, such as Medicare and subsidized or free prescription-drug benefits. Because of that, plus cost-of-living increases in benefits that have outstripped increases in payroll deductions, it is now being operated on a pay-as-you-go basis. The result? The supposed "dipping into the Trust Fund" (which we have already discussed) has always been done anyway. If this were honestly labeled, the claimed federal surplus under Clinton would have been far smaller, or maybe even in deficit.

Democratic Minnesota senator Paul Wellstone (since deceased) has asserted that Social Security "will be able to pay all promised benefits until 2038 without any changes." That sounds like good news, but even if it turns out to be true, all that means is that someone entering the workforce today can look forward to paying Social Security taxes for thirty-four years only to find there is nothing left when he/she retires.

This Trust Fund fantasy is worse than false—it is dangerous, because it creates a huge political obstacle to sensible, fiscal policy and lends itself to demagoguery. It has turned Social Security into the third rail of politics—touch it and your reelection hopes die a sudden death. You hope the system will hang together long enough that when you reach retirement age, others entering the system will be willing to pay enough in FICA taxes that you can be paid when you get to the top of the chain letter. You are totally dependent on a continuous flow of new money from those new workers entering the Social Security system.

GOOD MEDICINE: THE ENEMY OF THE SYSTEM

More people are living longer into their "golden years," and they vote in disproportionately high numbers, and this great voting bloc is treated very carefully by our legislators, who continue to increase their benefits faster than payroll deductions can rise. The irony is that medical advances that prolong life are actually an enemy of the system. An effective, widely accepted cancer cure or an end to heart disease would devastate it, because as they live longer than expected, each unanticipated recipient is a financial threat to the system. Even without that, too few will soon be paying for too many.

The baby boom of the forties and fifties, which brought a large number of workers into the system in the sixties and seventies, is about over, and fewer worker bees will enter the hive, while the number of recipients will increase enormously as 75 million baby boomers retire, starting in 2007–8. If the government continues to increase FICA deductions in order to maintain the appearance of solvency, the economy will grind to a halt because of this terrible drag on the purchasing power of the American worker.

Our senators and congressmen are pretty smart, however. They know how unsound the Social Security system is, so they have their own sound, healthy, fully funded pension program with generous cost-of-living escalators. Let me give you an example: When they retire, no matter how long they have been in office, they continue to draw their regular pay (unless increased by cost-of-living adjustments) until the day they die. It has been claimed by some that former senator Bill Bradley (D-NJ) and his wife can expect to draw $7.9 million over their lives, assuming they each have a normal life span. Whatever the total is, it costs them nothing! You and I pick up the tab. We would have to collect Social Security benefits for more than 46.5 years to do as well. I should live so long!

This leads to a suggestion that would trigger some honest changes—cancel Congress's wonderful plan for its members and put them only on Social Security, then watch them rush to fix the system! (Oops!! On second thought, they might just increase the payoff on the scam and place demands on it that would topple it sooner. Then they can continue to cynically vote for spending programs and more Social Security taxes and bigger monthly checks to buy votes because they are insulated from the problem they have caused. Just remember that the next time you vote for a "defender" of the Social Security system.)

I'm not so much worried that the Social Security system will collapse, but that the Social Security system will be the cause of the nation's bankruptcy (inflation), because it is the single largest obligation of government, and the unfunded liability defies description as discussed in chapter 2. The Social Security system's "unfunded obligations" (the excess promised to future recipients over the amount to be collected) will cost an unimaginable $39 trillion (2007 calculation) over the next seventy-five years. That's several times the expected output of the entire U.S. economy this year. The unfunded obligation grew from $20 trillion to $50 trillion since 2000, and is accelerating (see chapter 2).

Put another way, it's now a rotten deal getting worse every year. A worker who earned average wages and retired in 1980 at age 65 recovered the value of the retirement portion of his and his employer's "contribution," plus interest, in only 2.8 years. Every month he lived beyond that was pure gravy. It seemed like a pretty good deal for him, even if the return was only 2% per annum. However, those who retired at age 65 in 2000 will need 16.7 years to recover their money. If they die before age 81, they are shortchanged.

But you younger Americans who don't retire until 2025 will really take it in the shorts. It will take 27.4 years to get yours back. Just be sure not to die before age 93.

And that, of course, assumes that the system will still be alive and well then.

Why Social Security
Will Never Be Reformed

During the 2000 presidential campaign and the first few months of his administration, President Bush proposed that 2 percentage points of your FICA contribution be yours to invest in market securities at your option. Historically, that money would produce a return double the 2% yield you now get from Social Security and *the principal would be yours at retirement*! This proposal was immediately attacked by Gore and other Democrats as "a risky scheme," allegedly opened up to market risks, such as the bear market we are in as I write this.

Do you want to know the *real* reason why they opposed this fresh idea? It's because Social Security is a huge slush fund for government, and the big spenders will never let it out of their hands! Can you imagine what would happen to federal spending if all of a sudden the government could not borrow the Social Security Trust Fund and spend it on their favorite programs? They'd be at least $175 billion more short every year! But remember, the Fed has a printing press all primed to produce money. Inflation, anyone?

And what would happen if you could invest 2% of your FICA as you choose? There would simply be that much less money in the slush fund. And how "risky" is the scheme? That depends on what you invested the money in. If you invested it in Treasury securities or a T-bond fund, that is as close to riskless as you can get. Gold and silver are even better (see chapter 8).

SELF-FULFILLING PROPHECY?

I have been accused of undermining the very confidence in the system that keeps it alive by telling you this, but I trust the truth. What choice do I have? The present Social Security system is the *real* "risky scheme." Sooner or later the problems will be recognized, and this jury-rigged, dishonest system will collapse of its own weight, whether or not I talk about it. My concern is for you. You must plan your life on the sure premise that Social Security will be of very little help to you, and may have done you a lot of harm by discouraging saving, because it takes money away from you that you might have saved for yourself and gotten a return at least twice as high, and *you would also own the principal*. Also, most people believe that Social Security will "take care of me." That's what the AARP tells its members as it lobbies for more government benefits for senior citizens, and that's what our national legislators and political candidates tell us ad nauseam. They have made Social Security junkies out of us because even the most sophisticated financial planners seldom seriously question that Social Security will be there when needed.

Those who will be hurt most are those who were promised the most. The system is immoral, dishonest, and unethical, and we have bought the big lie and become hooked on it. The only honest way to save the system and the economy would be to slash benefits, which would not only be cruel at this point, but politically impossible. But the greater cruelty is yet to come when the system collapses of its own weight.

5

DON'T BANK ON IT

Just imagine you are the finance minister of a Middle East monarchy in the late seventies. You have to please your king, who has the power to cut off your hand (or your head) in the public square if he wishes. Your job is to see that he gets the maximum return from his billions in oil revenues. You have put his money into short-term deposits in New York banks, which, in turn, have loaned it out to insolvent countries. You thought this was a great idea at the time because that would leave the banks on the hook— responsible for both the loans they made and the money you deposited.

But now the prices of those things your king has been importing (heavy construction equipment, building materials, high technology, etc.) are inflating between 15 and 25% a year, so his dollars are getting chewed up by inflation. In addition, the dollar has been sinking against virtually every other currency in the world, and you are in the uncomfortable position of informing your monarch that he needs a 15 to 20% increase in oil prices just to break even.

If you think you feel sick now, look at your alternatives.

1. You can hedge your dollar losses by buying gold, which you have done covertly for some time anyway. As the dollar sinks, gold will keep rising and compensate for your losses, but there isn't enough gold around to hedge you against the monstrous number of dollars that you have earned and have to place somewhere. But you do what you can.

2. You can stay with the dollar and tough it out and hope that your ruler doesn't lose his patience during the several years you think it will take for the U.S. government to correct its balance-of-payments deficit, balance its budgets, and bring the dollar back to some semblance of strength—if ever. (They did so temporarily in the eighties and nineties.)

3. You can carefully pull your money out of the New York banks and throw it into some other currency, but you had better do it just right or you will throw the dollar and the U.S. banking system into a disastrous tailspin before you can get most of your money safely out, and your losses could be beyond imagining.

4. You can buy America, as China, Singapore, and others are now doing (buying part of Citibank, Merril Lynch, etc.).

The threat of withdrawal of Arab money from the New York banks is only one of several major potential banking problems we had to deal with in the seventies, when the first edition of this book was published. Our banking system is, to put it mildly, in still an increasingly vulnerable condition and racing toward the most serious test it has faced since the 1930s, if a not-unlikely combination of events should occur in the period from 2007 through 2010.

I think looking at a few banking fundamentals would be useful. Understanding the nature of the system might give us some guidance. Let's look at history.

In 1998, the five largest banking company mergers in U.S. history were all announced or completed. The largest of these—Travelers Group and Citicorp—resulted in a company with total assets of approximately $700 billion, more than double the assets of the largest U.S. banking company at the end of 1997. The combination of NationsBank and BankAmerica resulted in a company with total assets of approximately $572 billion. We were putting all our eggs in a few baskets. Bank of America and Citibank are two of the banks where nearly all of the thousands of smaller banks in the country do their banking. This is where all the money and credit in the U.S. come together. They are the key logs in the jam. If you pull out the log, the entire system crumbles. These banks make money by borrowing it from depositors at one rate and loaning it at a higher rate. The spread between these two interest rates (arbitrage) represents their profit. However, it's not really that simple, because the banks can, in effect, create money out of thin air, just as the United States government can.

Banks can get in trouble from both sides of their balance sheets:

1. Their outstanding loans could default (think subprime mortgages); or,

2. Their savings accounts and certificates of deposit (CDs) could be withdrawn (or not renewed) in a banking panic caused by cascading mortgage foreclosures, and, of course, that is the classic "run on the banks," as we've seen that only about 5% (or less) of their deposits are on hand in cash. The rest is loaned out or invested.

Banks operate on the assumption that all times are relatively normal and that nothing could ever happen that could endanger either their assets or their liabilities sufficiently to cause a "run" or abnormal loan losses. They count on public confidence and what one writer has called "the sticker principle." If you, as a depositor, ever got worried about your bank and decided to go down and take out your money, as you approach the door you would probably notice a small oval sticker that reads, "Deposits Insured to $100,000 by the Federal Deposit Insurance Corporation, an agency of the U.S. government." So you would say to yourself, "Well, perhaps I shouldn't worry. My account is less than $100,000, so Uncle Sam will protect me." So you leave your money there and go home.

Let's look at that protection and see how much it really covers.

The FDIC guarantees $4.116 trillion in bank deposits, based on current FDIC numbers (they insure only 60% of all deposits). The total amount of money in the FDIC insurance fund as of June 2006 was only $49.5 billion, and they have an open line of credit with the U.S. Treasury in case of an emergency (which is a promise to print money) if needed. That means there is only $1 of insurance coverage for every $83.33 on deposit, or stated another way, for every $1,000 you have in the bank, there is $12 to insure it if everyone were to draw on it at the same time. It would take only $49.5 billion (1.2% of the nation's deposits) to be wiped out through general banking failures, and the entire FDIC insurance fund would be penniless.

In 1975 the FDIC used over 40% of the total fund in the Franklin Bank failure rescue operation. Most of those funds have since been recovered, but what about the amount of money that was needed at the time of the problem? If a couple of the nation's top ten banks got in bad trouble, there wouldn't be nearly enough money in the FDIC fund to save them.

The good news is that not only is the government liable for $100,000 for each insured account (or $4.116 trillion), but it is the government's policy to cover every last dollar when a bank fails. This means the FDIC's $49.5 billion could be exhausted even more rapidly. Is the FDIC just being nice to us—going the extra mile?

The bad news is that if they call on the Treasury for more money, that guarantees much more inflation.

It was revealed by John Hensel, the FDIC regional administrator for national banks in the California region, at a seminar sponsored by Security National Bank (one of the banks that was on the Federal Reserve's problem list back in the seventies), that this generous policy was to compensate for the official policy of not disclosing the conditions of a problem bank to prevent runs and failures. The innocent public continues to open accounts at an insolvent bank, buy their CDs and their stock, not knowing of their troubles. If the bank goes under and the FDIC does not pay off 100%, it could be liable for huge damage suits from bamboozled depositors and innocent investors.

Hensel admitted that this could threaten the insurance fund since it has not been set up for such exposure.

In April 1974, FDIC chairman Frank Wille admitted that the FDIC had no way of foreseeing a banking problem, saying, "We are trying to develop a classification system which will tell whether a particular banking institution, previously unclassified, may have become a 'problem bank' since it was last examined." And they are no closer to making that "classification" system solvent now than they were then. Mr. Wille assured us that, in regard to the FDIC rescue funds, "We could handle several large bank failures." And he hastily backed off, "But not a general run on the banks."

That ought to be an eye-opener, especially when one considers who said it. If you don't think a general run on the bank is possible, listen to what Mr. Wille had to say shortly after that. "Like it or not, the nation's banks are all affected by any significant failures that occur within the banking system." Sen. William Proxmire, former chairman of the Senate Banking Committee, said on February 1, 1976, "A relatively limited economic setback could result, conceivably, in the failure of some of the nation's largest banks." When one bank goes down the tubes, if it is big enough, it can take other banks with it. The international banking panic of the 1930s began with the failure of a small bank in Austria. Banks borrow short-term from one another, and they honor checks drawn on other banks, and allow depositors to draw on those checks before they have cleared the issuing banks. A sudden and abrupt failure of a major bank could produce chaos at the clearinghouses and have a devastating effect on all banks.

But the real uncertainty occurs when depositors become aware of bank problems and begin to react with general concern about the banking system. In a real panic, they won't distinguish between sound or unsound banks. All banks could become suspect. The only thing that prevents people from doing it is their belief that the banks cannot fail.

On April 21, 1975, *Business Week* observed that:

The banking system's problems are serious with an over-hang of very shaky loans the most visible ones. 'Last summer scared the pants off some of these bankers,' says John Pop-pen of Booz Allen Hamilton, the management consultants. Banks, and such nonbanking holding company subsidiaries as finance companies, leasing companies, mortgage bankers, and real-estate investment trusts literally funded everyone that needed money in the last decade. They used up their own deposits, and then sold CDs and holding company commercial paper, and borrowed federal funds to keep the game going, creating loan/deposit and capital/asset ratios that were simply intolerable.

The risk got so great that banks in 1974 had to charge off an unprecedented $1.8 billion to cover loan losses, and there are still billions of dollars in loans in considerable trouble—$10 to $12 billion in loans to real-estate investment trusts [1976 numbers, thirty-one years ago. It's much worse now.].

The generation of bankers that rose to power in the early 1960s has never known a truly sick economy. They took their ability to survive the minor economic disturbances of the 1960s as proof they could survive anything.

Problems in 1974 pulled things apart. Inflation turned strong demand for bank money into frenzied demand, but more lend-ing forced the banks to borrow still more, and by mid-1974 the system was stretched dangerously thin: Too much ques-tionable lending, too much borrowed money, and too little capital to support swollen assets and monetary growth. . . .

And that was three decades ago. Think subprime mort-gages today.

In 1975, if the comptroller of the currency had required the banks to mark down all of their assets to market value, there would have been no capital left in the banks of America, and they would have been technically and legally insolvent and forced to shut down. Can you imagine what happened to the market value of their bond portfolios when interest rates soared to 18% in 1981? (Bond prices go down when interest rates rise.) And yet they were carried on the books at the purchase price or par value, and survived because of deception.

They loaned much more than $100 billion to insolvent countries, either directly or through their foreign subsidiaries, and then made further loans, either directly or through the International Monetary Fund and the World Bank, just so those countries could stay current on their interest payments, and technically those loans would be carried on the books as "good loans."

The strong recovery in the eighties from the recession of the seventies, and the massive injections of capital in 2000 after the dot.com collapse that year, temporarily saved the system, and soon earnings were looking pretty good again. But one more big event might raise the risks for several of our biggest banks to unacceptable levels, and inflation is one villain, rising interest rates is another, and subprime mortgage and ARM defaults is another.

When inflation rises, interest rates climb, so everyone gets mad at the banks for "profiteering," but bear in mind that it also causes huge losses in the market value of their bond portfolios. Also, when general interest rates rise well above the rates that banks are willing to pay on deposits, a process called "disintermediation" sets in. Depositors withdraw money from the banks looking for higher yields elsewhere, and they can find them in such relatively safe investments as Treasury bills or money-market funds. This is a form of "bank run."

Here are the banking danger areas:

1. **A modern-day run on the banks.** One or two top-twenty banks could get into serious public trouble, as people withdraw deposits and refuse to renew CDs at maturity, looking for higher yields, safety, and capital gains, probably in gold, silver, foreign currencies, and U.S. T-bonds. If it were widely publicized, this could result in a panicky stampede.

2. **Billions in foreign loans** to countries that would have defaulted long ago if further loans had not been made to them so they could make their interest payments. One of those unstable countries could undergo a coup d'état by al-Qaeda or other Islamic radicals who would refuse to honor the debt, claiming Koranic prohibitions against "usury" or perhaps a group of the poorer debtor countries might get together and say, "We want a larger piece of the world's wealth or we will default on our bank loans."

3. **A rash of recession/inflation-caused big corporate bankruptcies** (possibly Bear Stearns?), to say nothing of mortgage defaults. This is precisely what we will see in the next recession, and this could be the triggering mechanism for a full-fledged bank panic.

4. **China or India giving up on the dollar.** They could try to switch into euros, deutsche marks, Swiss francs, Japanese yen, gold, commodities, and American real estate at depressed prices, or buying up American banks and brokerage firms, rather than invest in short-term deposits in the money-center banks, as they do now.

Through a Glass Darkly

The true condition of the money-center banks is difficult to determine as so much of their business is done through overseas subsidiaries that generally do not have U.S. reporting requirements. We do know that the largest multinational banks like Bank of America, Chase, and Citibank have approximately 60% of their loans and over 60% of their earnings from overseas, and in foreign currencies. They are truly "citizens of the world." They don't just use the world's monetary system, they *are* the world's monetary system, and to determine their true status is not easy.

Forbes on July 24, 1975, devoted its issue to an analysis of the banks from an investor's point of view. "Banks do not have to disclose as much about their operations as most other companies do. The idea has always been that public confidence in bank deposits is more important than investor confidence in their stocks. Information that might lead investors to sell their stock might also frighten depositors into pulling out their money. A declining stock market is one thing; a bank panic is something else again. Anything that might set off a bank panic is something to be discouraged.

"That policy, which both the Federal Reserve and the Comptroller of the Currency support, is, of course, vehemently opposed by the S.E.C. . . ."

Investors are suspicious. Analyst John Lyons, of the bank-stock firm of Keefe, Bruyette & Woods, observes that New York bank profits in the aggregate were up 30% in 1975, but that, "Potential loan losses are an absolute unknown, and in specific cases they could wipe out earnings." The FDIC, Federal Reserve, and comptroller of the currency were so concerned about the extent of the problem in 1976 and the disclosure thereof that they successfully defied a congressional subpoena demanding disclosure of federal records of all U.S. banks with more than $1 billion in assets.

The recent monstrous transfer of dollars to China and India has not totally destroyed the dollar, only because they were recycling their profits back into this country, mostly through buying U.S. Treasury securities. They don't even have to pull their money out in order to destabilize us. All they have to do is stop pouring money in, and that may have begun as this is written. Most of these problems can be papered over as long as inflation is under control, but when it breaks loose, any or all of these problems can become critical, and the banks and the Treasury could be assaulted from every direction at once.

First, the federal government will have to mount a huge rescue operation. It will print, if necessary, hundreds of billions of dollars to help the banks meet the demand from depositors. More inflation pressures! The banks could also invoke their right to refuse to give you your money upon demand, if they really need to, but it would take years to restore confidence again. The following statement of policy is pretty typical of most banks: "Depositor(s) may at any time be required by Bank to give notice of an intended withdrawal, not less than 60 days before a withdrawal is made. The intent of this provision is to protect the best interests of the Bank and depositors alike, and it will be enforced only in cases of financial excitement or when it may be deemed expedient by the Bank's Board of Directors" (First National Bank of McMinnville, Tennessee).

They can also stave off defeat for a few days by declaring a " bank holiday." Under various Executive Orders issued by the president, the government can freeze all transfers of funds from the banks, pleading "national emergency." At best, it would mean great inconvenience for you as you would have to wait for your money. At worst, it could mean no acceptable means of exchange and the total loss of your money. By the time you get it, it may not be worth much.

Now, you have some practical problems. What should you do? I don't know when the banks are going to be in trouble, or even if they will go broke for sure. I don't know how soon after publication you will read this book, or how far along the road things will be by the time you get your hands on it. All I know is that the risks can be high. If, on any given day, only 5% of the depositors of the banks demanded their funds, even the strongest banks could fail. Obviously, conditions would have to deteriorate substantially before this kind of panic could happen, but we've already learned that inflation is precisely what can cause this. So here are my recommendations, based on what was learned in the close call with the economic grim reaper in the 1970s:

1. Don't buy bank CDs. Only a small amount of money needed for the orderly conduct of your financial affairs should be kept either in your checking account or in demand-deposit savings accounts or a money-market mutual fund. The T-bill market will be the last market to go broke, and that would give you time to get your funds out. T-bills are the equivalent of cash. Most of your assets should be in the countercyclical investments that we will discuss later. Your bank deposits will be battered by inflation at best anyway, so why accept the risks of the banking system?

2. Don't worry about whether your bank is a good one or a bad one. If your bank is small and one of the first to fall, the FDIC will probably rescue it, and you will merely go to the bank one day and find that it has been merged with another bank through secret negotiations with the FDIC and the comptroller of the currency, and you will be able to get your money without any difficulty. It's when the entire system is in danger and shuts down for a while that everyone is in trouble, regardless of what bank you patronize.

Safe-Deposit Boxes

3. Is a safe-deposit box really safe? It had better be. The contents are my property, not those of the bank, and can't be attached by the banks' creditors, unless you have a loan in default at the same bank or a delinquent bank credit card account. Your bank deposits and CDs can and will be lost if enough banks are in sufficient trouble to overwhelm the FDIC. But safe-deposit box contents are yours. The government in a crisis can seize any cash, gold, silver, and firearms from your safe-deposit box, but everything else is yours.

If the banking system should go broke, you may have trouble getting to your box because the doors will be shut, and there may be crowds. But after the dust settles and the panic is over, you will have access to your box. Maintain a separate inventory of everything for insurance purposes. If you have a joint account, don't keep your will there because in many states it is illegal to remove anything in the case of a death of one of the co-owners until appropriate authorization from the courts. Your will should be on file with your attorney or in a safe place at home.

4. The banks most likely to reopen after a panic are the flagship banks of the big banking groups. The nation will have to restore a monetary system of some kind, and it can only do it through the banking system, and those are the ones that would represent the highest degree of safety for your necessary dealings, even though they happen to be the ones that are most exposed to some of the bad loans. But remember, again, even if the bank doesn't go broke, the money may.

Up-to-Date Concerns

Some of these examples so far are in the past, from the first edition of this book, and the banking system has managed to sail safely through, sometimes just pulling back from the edge of the precipice. But there is a current deadly threat you should know about that could deliver the coup de grace—the bursting real estate bubble. With the recent (and possibly current) decline of the value of homes, not only is home equity in danger of being whittled away by falling residential real estate prices, but the banks are really exposed.

After the dot.com collapse in 2000, the Fed lowered interest rates to below 1 percent and flooded the system with money to prevent the general stock market collapse from cascading into a recession, or even a depression. They kept those interest rates artificially low (near zero) for several years. During that time, individuals created a vulnerable real estate bubble. Two things are different about this real estate boom compared to any others before now:

1. There was also a huge burst of refinancing, which is not necessarily bad if the money was used productively, but much of it went into consumer spending, which partly accounts for the Bush economic recovery. Much of the

boom that Bush fans are touting was caused by consumer spending of money raised from refinancing. The subsequent collapse of the residential real estate bubble ate away at those equities, and suddenly many homes were below water, with the loan balance bigger than the house was worth.

2. Some innovative types of mortgages had hidden time bombs for the borrowers. I am referring to ARMs. These mortgages had cheap, teaser starter rates, making it possible for many homeowners to afford these rates and buy a home who could not have otherwise qualified for a mortgage. The hidden time bomb was down the road. If interest rates went up, even a little, these mortgage interest rates would rise, increasing the monthly payments to where many people could no longer pay. This would trigger a rising tide of unaffordable mortgages and foreclosures.

Now the plot thickens. Wall Street and the bankers decided to "securitize" these loans. They pooled the loans into bonds, with these loans as collateral. Because the bonds were believed to be fully collateralized, they got good credit ratings; a lot of big investors and banks bought them, thinking they would be safe because of their collateral and their deceptively high credit ratings. But the hidden devil finally showed his fangs. When the foreclosures of these loans began, holders of these bonds found that their good credit rating was a farce. The foreclosures began with the "subprime" loans, which were granted to borrowers sucked in by the low starter rates whose credit and assets would not have qualified them in the past if there had not been a flood of money available and the deceptively low rates on their ARMs. Often there was no down payment.

As these bonds started to erode due to rising foreclosures on their collateral, a lot of them were held by banks, and large investors began, with justification, to worry. Soon they were selling the bonds, and the whole system began to break down. One fund, managed by Bear Stearns, suffered from bad fore-closure rates in the bond collateral; in fact, it has endangered the very existence of that huge broker.

This process is still in its early stages as this is written, as the real estate decline has migrated from the subprime loans to even "prime" loans and "good credit" loans, and as the rising tide of foreclosed, vacant homes on the market affected everyone, even those with good credit, if homes with sub-prime loans began to be vacant and for sale in their town or neighborhood. In St. George, Utah, where Kay and I lived for a few years, historically there were usually 300 homes for sale before 2006. Now, in 2007, there are more than 3,000. As a result, prices have collapsed. The law of supply/demand has triumphed again. This bursting real estate bubble is now bursting nationwide, and as this edition is written, I believe it has at least two or three declining years to run. The threat to the banking system from crumbling bonds secured by weak mortgages is immense. The threat to brokers and the banks that hold the mortgage or the securitized bonds is now obvious.

I don't know what the outcome will be, but this could be the push that tips over some weak banks and has a domino ef-fect. We could get lucky like banks in the seventies and work through these problems without a general collapse, but it is a deadly threat to the system. I don't know what other threats will materialize, but the banks are not as safe as everyone thinks, and the FDIC bailout fund is far smaller than will be necessary to deal with the potential problems.

So, don't bank on it!

I don't know that the banks will suddenly go broke. That would be foolish. I just want you to know how vulnerable the banks are to the inevitable financial earthquakes, and that the risks will rise as inflation accelerates and/or real estate prices continue to erode. There are many better ways to earn money than by putting it in the bank, and there are many safer places to put your money. It is foolish to give them any more of your money than necessary. As we have seen, if you loan a bank your money at 5% or less, you are getting ripped off by inflation, and if you spend the interest, you are consuming your capital. Keep as much distance from the banks as you possibly can. They may be dangerous to your financial health.

6

SIN TAX

John Adams once said that, "Our Constitution was made only for a moral and religious people. It is wholly inadequate to the government of any other." What does that have to do with money, economics, and survival? A heck of a lot. Any society's economy must be interpreted within the framework of its social systems. What John Adams meant was that this nation was based upon shared values (which are also shared by many who are not "religious"). Edmund Burke elaborated still further on this principle: "Men of intemperate habits cannot be free. Their passions form their fetters."

This nation has worked because there was a general consensus that we had a responsibility to the general good and that every man was responsible for his personal welfare, that individuals were to be charitable to those who were unable to care for themselves, and there was no sympathy for those who would not work. We were willing to take up arms to defend our country. We believed that we could pull ourselves up by our own bootstraps and that life rewarded those who struggled. We looked up to those who achieved and did not punish success by excessive taxation. We were willing to sacrifice security for the opportunities that complete freedom offered us—along with the risks. People avoided "the dole" because to be dependent was humiliating, and this attitude motivated great achievements and was a strength to society in general.

We believed in secure, stable money, and several times through hard experience we have learned what happens when we violate this principle, as our currency system has collapsed more than once, but the effects were relatively muted in the past because of the higher degree of decentralization and independence.

There was a general consensus as to what was "right" and "wrong" in ethics and morals. The traditional family was honored as the time-tested basic structural unit of society, and the "three generation family" was the mainstay of our society.

I could go on and on about basic structural changes. It is the intangible, "spiritual" consensus that determines the strength of the society. This nation will become ungovernable as this consensus dwindles. I agree with John Adams that our Constitution is "wholly inadequate to the government" of any people who do not, in a general consensus, accept these basic principles. Our founding fathers operated on the principle that true freedom requires voluntary restraint.

I would like to address one area in which this consensus is becoming unraveled, and zero in on those areas that are most likely to give society changes that are beyond your ability to adapt to, cope with, or pay for.

The Sexual Revolution

The sexual revolution represents a great threat to our economy. It may be the one factor that can cause all of my optimistic forecasts of economic recovery from our inflationary ills to go astray.

Every society has basic structural factors that everyone takes for granted and must remain stable. In *Fiddler on the Roof*, Tevye understood this when he sang about tradition. Everyone in his society had a role and knew that role and performed it well, so they had a stable and balanced society. And when new (even positive) values came into the society too rapidly, their little village crumbled around their ears, helped, of course, by outside forces.

The changing value that concerns me as an economic factor most is the sexual revolution because it is an assault upon the basic nurturing and cohesive unit of society—the family—and it has financial consequences that are awesome to contemplate. Professor Urie Bronfenbrenner, of the Psychology Department of Cornell University, once observed that "the American family is falling apart." He said that thirty-five years ago, and that scary trend is many times worse today. Violence and vandalism are rampant in our schools, and more people are living alone, and these disturbing trends must be reversed if we are to survive as a nation. "Changes of this magnitude have occurred before in times of great national upheavals like wars, depressions and floods. The family will either become more important again or we will go down the drain like Greece and Rome did. As soon as the family fell apart in Greece and Rome, so did the whole society."

Now what does the family have to do with money?

In a traditional family structure where parents are faithful to each other and devoted to their children, societies remain stable. Families stay together, and divorce is infrequent. Basic reverence for family and ancestors maintained relative social stability for centuries in Japan and Germany. The nuclear family was the basic motivating force in the colonization and development of our country. The sexual revolution is an assault upon that institution.

I have long been convinced that the religious restrictions against extramarital or premarital sex, which are common to the Christian and Hebrew Scriptures, are more for the protection of society than for the regulation of the life of the individual. If you stop to consider it, it becomes apparent that all of the rules of sexual behavior, such as the rules against incest and adultery, seem to be designed to prevent sexual rivalry within or outside the family, which leads to broken families. The laws against premarital sex are designed to prevent children from being brought into the world without a stable "nuclear family" environment to nurture them.

These were reasonable, rational attempts to control behavior for the greater good of the society. Whether you believe they were man-made or inspired by God, they are wise laws.

To sum it up, much of what organized religion called "sin" is a set of essential behavioral standards, the violation of which will destabilize society. This is not a simple matter of opinion or a moralistic position. As we shall see from some of the statistics, violation of these standards leads to fiscal instability, confiscatory taxation, and inflationary ruin. We have no choice but to study human moral and ethical behavior, along with traditional economics, when we try to understand the present and forecast the future.

SEX, FAMILY, AND TAXES

Throughout history, advanced civilizations have had very restrictive, somewhat puritanical sexual codes during their ascendency and peak. Codes of sexual behavior were sometimes "honored in the breach," but even when they were being violated, it was understood that a common standard was being violated. Civilizations in decline tend to reach the point where the violation becomes the common, socially acceptable behavior among the upper and middle classes.

The traditional family is not only the child-rearing unit of society, it is the means by which the values of one generation are passed on to the next, and by which the inexperienced young are protected against the consequences of their inevitable errors in judgment. The quality of the family determines whether succeeding generations will be neurotic, criminal, unstable, and a burden to society, or whether they will be strong, responsible, moral, independent, and emotionally and spiritually stable contributors to society. When we train our children, we are, in effect, training our grandchildren. Adultery brings jealousy and sexual rivalry, which can poison or break up the family unit, or at the very least make it a loveless environment to raise a child.

Adultery is *always* as much an integrity problem as it is a sexual "sin," because the adulterer has to lie, sneak around, and violate his most sacred promises. I don't believe anyone can have a deceitful double life without suffering spiritual and emotional damage, which has to reflect itself in tensions in the home. When society relaxes its attitudes against premarital, extramarital, or nonmarital sex, as we have done today, there is an explosion of unmarried family units without long-term legal and emotional commitments. In 2003, there were more than 4.6 million such unmarried family units.

I have noticed with great interest that the climbing divorce rate has flattened out. Don't get too thrilled with that. It's simply because the most unstable elements of our society that are most likely to divorce are the ones starting those unmarried household units, and they are the ones that will break up, leaving fatherless or motherless children, and no statistical tracks.

I know what it is like to grow up without a father. My dad died when I was six months old and I never knew him. When I became a father, I had no role model. I had to learn how to do it all by myself. The result was a lot of mistakes while I was learning, despite my good intentions. When society condones casual sexual relationships that create children without a father role model, with little girls being starved for male affection and little boys not experiencing "father-son male bonding," the end result is generally promiscuity, illegitimacy, and its accompanying burdens on society. Society ends up paying the bill.

I think I turned out okay, and I'm sure others did also, but the odds were against us.

Loosening sexual morality always ends up hitting society in its pocketbook. The exponential growth of taxes to support unwed mothers and children without fathers (welfare costs) can be directly traced to the sexual revolution, and it is the major contributing factor leading to juvenile crime, alcoholism, abortions, drug addiction, and disrupted schools that can no longer teach, but can only "police," and badly, too. And you pay for it!

This raises an interesting question. Does society have a right to enforce its traditional morality bylaws as a protective measure to save itself, if that enforcement interferes with the human right to "sin"? The answer to that question is that if the majority of the people in a society have chosen to violate these stabilizing standards, passing laws won't help. Again, we get back to John Adams's invisible consensus. The key factor was everyone's agreement that certain areas of life could not be regulated by law, and that these areas would be responsibly regulated by the people themselves. When the people cease to regulate themselves, society finds it impossible to come up with fair laws that are acceptable to society, and society and its individuals are the losers. To attempt to control human sexual behavior by law raises grave questions, while at the same time, to permit the flouting of aberrant behavior and give it social respectability raises equally grave questions, and I feel threatened no matter what we do. That is why hating homosexuals is profoundly disturbing to me. Homosexuality is an assault on the family institution, which I strongly oppose, but laws attacking homosexuality are an assault on freedom, and personal hatred of gays is always wrong, and I feel in jeopardy when social trends have placed society in a position of having to choose between condoning a nontraditional family lifestyle and personally attacking homosexuals. So we have a classic example of rights in conflict.

In my opinion, any society that does not sustain a general consensus that sex is reserved for heterosexual marriage and old-fashioned morals will reap a harvest of unstable, confused children and relationships that shift like the sands, leaving children the bewildered, twisted victims. But if Adams's invisible consensus has broken down, a free democratic society cannot enforce laws regarding sexual behavior without becoming a police state.

In my church counseling responsibilities, I've seen over and over again how the lack of an effective role model for children leads to unstable second and third generations. Marriage is a tough enough learning ground for amateurs, even with a role model. As our children marry, they will be able to look back on a loving and stable relationship between and with their parents. I hope they learned from me how to be a father and leader in the home and how to love, respect, and cherish a spouse. I hope they will have learned from Kay how to deal with stress and disagreement in a mature way, with my support, and how to raise children in a firm and loving manner.

All we can really do to insulate ourselves is to create oases of sexual stability and fidelity in our homes and churches. If we don't, the next unstable generation will bleed us dry in welfare costs, crime, drug addiction, alcoholism, violence, police costs, fire costs, legal fees, and gigantic and expensive government efforts to deal with these problems. If we sow the wind, we will reap the whirlwind.

For example, between 2000 and 2003, 30% of all newborn babies in this country were born to a single parent. According to Peter Schuck, a deputy assistant secretary of HEW, "There is definitely a high correlation between out-of-wedlock births, welfare costs and many of our most pressing social problems." Too often the children run wild for lack of supervision, and mothers become mired in a life of poverty, crime, alcoholism, drug addiction, and child abuse. Psychologist Bronfenbrenner says, "These people are going to put a growing burden on our society, not only to sustain them but to repair the social and economic damage they do."

Back in the late seventies, the Carter administration offered a new bill on adolescent pregnancy prevention and care that would finance more counseling, contraceptives, classes, and day care for pregnant unwed teenagers, which then cost at least $60 million a year. That brought to $344 million the total that HEW asked Congress to spend on teenage pregnancy, starting in the seventies. The total current cost in tax dollars is impossible to determine, but it is safe to say it adds up to thousands per taxpaying family per year. A society that collectively makes wrong decisions in these areas is a society on a collision course with financial and social disaster, to say nothing of the moral and religious implications. No moral authority can be exercised (over a society) that is not voluntarily granted to its leadership by its citizens, regardless of laws.

Based on the above principles, just on economic grounds, let alone moral grounds, I am violently opposed to pornography, sexually explicit films and television, and bringing children into the world without the emotional and legal commitments of marriage. I am especially concerned about publications advocating the "new morality," such as *Playboy*, *Penthouse*, and so on, which have gained such respectability that you can buy them in almost any drugstore or 7-Eleven in America. Their publishers have paid premium prices to get respectable authors to write articles on serious subjects to provide the rationale that many people need in order to justify buying sexually explicit material. Their very respectability makes them more dangerous, in my opinion, than the grossest hard-core pornography, because it is so generally available in places that are considered respectable.

I am concerned about the consequences of a man moving into middle age, who every day is comparing his wife, as she adds wrinkles and pounds as the years, childbearing, and gravity take their toll, with the forever-young, physically perfect, airbrushed centerfold, and decides that his loyal spouse cannot measure up to this fantasyland ideal. No woman can compete with that, and it may well be that this fantasy is the reason for much male sexual dissatisfaction and infidelity, and for much unhappiness in the home.

Fortunately, sometimes the pendulum swings both ways. The 1920s were a period of great sexual license and rapid moral change. Isadora Duncan, with her free-love philosophy, was a great heroine back then. The movies were very explicit for their times, and there was a very large underground market for hard-core pornography. When we went into the Depression of the thirties, however, most everyone became concerned with the fundamentals of barely eking out an existence, and the nation swung into a puritanistic backlash in our schools, the movies, and the arts. Illicit sex had to go underground, where it belonged. This puritanical period lasted almost twenty-five years.

The good news is that the age in which we find ourselves may be just another swing of the pendulum, albeit considerably worse than the twenties. We hope the pendulum will swing back when we go into the next crash, because people simply will not have the time, leisure, or emotional energy for the kind of hedonism with which we live now.

By now you understand the fundamental concept of the economic consequences of sin. It was really brought home to me when I had to spend about $15,000 over the years caring for three children of a woman friend of our family who had joined the sexual revolution. These children, who were illegitimate and brought up without a father, ended up in our laps, as she simply could not keep her family together for a variety of reasons, and came to Kay and me for help. Her sexual behavior had a price tag for me. We have had more than thirty foster children in our home for various lengths of time, and in many instances there were sexual problems in their homes.

It is a national tragedy to know that more than 40% of the babies born in this country have no father in the home, and nearly all of them will end up being wards of the city, state, and/or country, and the direct and indirect costs have to be numbered in the hundreds of billions of dollars and eventually in the trillions, not to mention the enormous waste of precious human potential. And if that isn't an economic issue, I don't know what is.

PART 2

SURVIVING IN STYLE

We've wallowed in trouble long enough. I don't deliberately set out to be pessimistic, but it would be foolish to be unrealistic. These dark clouds all have silver linings only an optimist can see, and someone had to define the problem. You must be aware of the problems, or you won't act. We all need some personal and financial defensive positions. I don't expect to have a fire in my house, but I expect to have a fire drill. I don't expect to crash my car, but I own insurance.

These problems do not necessarily mean the end of Western civilization. I've said it before and I'll say it again, I believe the nation will recover. I know that some media reviewers will choose to misinterpret this as a "doom and gloom" book and will never read it, but will concentrate on "the Coming Bad Years" in the title because that gets attention. I must make it clear that I am as persuaded of the ability of the country to survive all these problems as I am of the problems themselves. The function of this book is to help each family get across the gulf of those bad years, and you won't do that unless you can clearly see the potential danger and prepare for it.

Not only is there a silver lining in this cloud as far as our government and our nation is concerned, but there are silver linings for you personally. Every one of those problems has within itself the seeds of personal solutions for you and your family.

Let's repeat what Will Rogers said. "Invest in inflation; it's the only thing that's going up." Whether or not inflation is good or bad for you depends on whether or not you own some of those things that are inflating in price. If some of your assets are invested in those things that do well during inflationary spirals, you are personally insulated from the worst effects. I can't pretend you will escape all of the effects of a national or worldwide depression because you will be exposed to increased crime, possible civil disorders, and even dangers to the Constitution itself. And obviously that will affect all of us, no matter how rich we might be, but over the long haul, as we fight our way through these problems, I am convinced that we can stand on the right side of the financial balance sheet and end up with our assets intact, as well as our personal health and safety. If you have a reasonable amount of self-sufficiency, if the distribution machine misses a few beats, you'll be okay.

Part II, now coming up, deals with the most fundamental aspect of my total program. This may be the only relevant advice for some of you, because 1) some of you won't have enough money to go beyond it; and 2) some of you have taken the financial moves already, having perceived these problems, but you haven't dealt with the survival steps.

I will now discuss personal survival and safety. Be sure you do not overreact to the realities. There are a lot of "gloom and doom" guys out there who would have you bail out of society and get a place in the mountains with a machine gun turret on the roof. I believe that is dumb and unnecessary.

So let's move on to a sensible plan that does not burn your bridges behind you and gives you some flexible alternatives if my timetable is off, or if it doesn't turn out exactly as I think. It's possible to be right about the problem but miss the boat in judging the implications. The program must be flexible and you must grasp the principles that will enable you to adapt your strategy to changing situations over the years. But the advice in part II will not change. It's fundamental advice that I would give you, even if the odds favored good times ahead.

I originally published this section in Edition I in 1977, and it has survived the years pretty much intact in this second edition; the principles still apply.

7

PANIC PROOF

And now, here comes Ruff's Recommendation Number 1. Store enough food and other basic commodities for six months. Survival starts here.

In June 1978, I was one of several speakers at a monetary conference in the Bahamas, sponsored by the National Committee for Monetary Reform. The speakers included Harry Browne, Harry Schultz, and Richard Russell, among others, all of whom I respect greatly because they are nearly all of the same "hard money" economic persuasion. One after another they trotted out their scenarios of serious economic problems. Some felt that we were headed for a hyperinflation, and others felt that we were headed for a deflationary depression similar to the 1930s. (By now you know where I stand on that issue.) All of them predicted some kind of monetary collapse, and they all made investment recommendations. Not one attempted to deal with the practical problems we all would have faced if these scenarios had come true. I stood in front of that group of eight hundred people and asked a simple question.

"How many of you believe that we're headed for some kind of monetary chaos?" Nearly every hand in the room went up. I then followed up with one more question: "Do you honestly believe in a period of monetary collapse that you will be able to safely drive down to your supermarket in your gas-guzzling car, make a selection from a dazzling variety of goods on the shelf, pay for them with your personal check, walk safely out the door to your car, drive home, and put them in your dependable, electric-operated refrigerator?"

That's the first time I ever got an ovation for a question— after a moment of reflective silence.

I simply cannot for the life of me understand how people can recognize our potential problems and somehow believe that the marketplace will still function normally in all cases. The marketplace is a hardy weed and it's pretty hard to kill off. It's not that there will be no marketplace. I'm saying that it may not function dependably, and it is likely there will be some periods of disruption. There may be times when there is food available, but not what you would prefer to eat. You might have to stand in line for scarce goods. There is a distinct possibility of labor troubles upsetting transportation; in fact, I think it is a probability. Historically during periods of runaway inflation, organized labor fights hard to keep up its spending power, and their only weapon is the strike. There will also be rumors that will panic people into running for any food they can get their hands on.

Back in 1962, I was driving through the eastern Colorado prairies on a business trip when I turned on my radio and heard President Kennedy announcing the Cuban missile crisis. When he told us that he had put the Strategic Air Command on alert, my stomach turned over, and an actual physical chill spread through my body. I stopped at the first service station and called my wife and asked her if we had any food in the house. That's a rather embarrassing question for a Mormon to ask, as we're supposed to have at least a six-month supply of food. But back in those days, we just didn't feel we had the money to do it (no excuse, of course). When she said we didn't have very much, I told her to go down to the supermarket and buy everything she could with whatever money she had.

When I got home, I found that the stores were jammed with people buying everything in sight. Many supermarkets in Denver were literally stripped of anything edible, while newspapers reported fights and some minor rioting as everyone translated that frightening news into personal action to provide some security. Food was their first instinctive response.

I had another example of the "fear syndrome" when we had a meat shortage in California in the early seventies. There was the darnedest panic buying you ever saw. One day I stopped at the supermarket to pick up some groceries for my wife. I was walking by the meat tray, which was an empty, glistening chrome wasteland. Suddenly one of the clerks came up with a cartful of plastic-wrapped packages of hamburger and dumped them in the tray in front of me. There must have been an announcement made over the store's PA system that I didn't hear, because as I reached for some to take home, I found myself literally swarmed under by a crowd of pushing, gouging, elbowing women, all grabbing for hamburger. Being caught up in the general hysteria, I began grabbing all I could get (doing my share of pushing and elbowing) and charged off to the checkout counter with my arms full. After I paid for the ten packages of hamburger I had managed to corner, I suddenly realized I didn't even like that store's hamburger that much. I had been caught up in a small panic, and I didn't like what happened to me.

Perception is as bad as reality in its effect on the marketplace. There's an old adage in the stock market that says, "Buy on rumor, sell on news." Johnny Carson created a toilet paper shortage that lasted for over a month when he told a joke about such a possible shortage on his TV show.

Gustave Le Bon wrote a book called *The Crowd: A Study of the Popular Mind*, in which he described the mob psychology, and it could be very instructive reading today. In my opinion, the American people swing between total apathy on the one hand, with a lack of perception of any of these problems (or at least an unwillingness to admit them), and overreaction on the other hand.

This chapter is designed to panic-proof your life. I think we should start where we and the system are most vulnerable, and that happens to be food. You're vulnerable because you can't do without it. It would only take two days to be very uncomfortable, and three or four days to create real suffering, and a week or ten days to produce severe health problems. Food is perishable, and the distribution system is the most sensitive to disruption.

I don't believe we will ever have an African or Asian-type famine in this country, with people dropping dead in the streets. We will always produce enough food in the vast agricultural areas of California and the Midwest to feed our people. We could have a 60% failure of our wheat and corn crops and still feed ourselves, as we export that much. But if such an event occurred, prices would go sky-high and you might be reduced to a bare subsistence diet because of skyrocketing prices. However, it is the disruption of the monetary system that represents the largest threat.

In the sixties and seventies we were subjected to pitiful newspaper pictures of small children with matchstick arms and legs and distended bellies in places with such names as Biafra, Somalia, and the Sahel. It seems that in this world of incredible abundance and surpluses, people are starving. In Ethiopia, untold tens of thousands of people have died and children have had their physical and mental growth permanently stunted from lack of protein and sufficient calories in their diet. And strangely enough, this happened in the face of the fact that the world generally is producing more food than it can consume, and can produce several times more. The United States and other prosperous nations were more than willing to send more food to Africa, and did so. It arrived safely in the port cities, but the people still starved. African politics and distribution systems weren't prepared to deal with such political problems, and political intrigue made pawns of dying people.

This is a simple, tragic example of how famines are generally political, social, and economic in nature rather than related to natural disasters. The creeping desert in north-central Africa is largely a result of the way man has treated the land, by overgrazing and poor farming techniques, but there is still no need for anyone in this world to be hungry, based on the amount of food available.

The problem is politics, distribution, and money.

We prosperous Americans, surrounded by wasteful abundance, never question the assumption that "it could never happen here," but if our economy is disrupted, those mountains of surplus wheat in the silos of the Midwest could be just as far away from us as the grain rotting in warehouses in Addis Ababa is from those children who need it so desperately.

Bear with me while I make a point in a rather circuitous manner.

In 1964, I bought an airplane for business use and learned to fly. Later, someone convinced me I'd be a lot safer if I had two engines instead of one, so we went out and bought a very expensive twin-engine Beechcraft Baron, under the assumption that if one engine quit, I could always fly home on the good engine. Great idea, but after I bought the aircraft I made an interesting discovery.

When you have two engines, you have more than doubled the complexity. Complexity creates vulnerability, so there is several times the chance of something going wrong. Surprisingly, the rate of fatal accidents is higher in twin-engine aircraft than it is with singles (if you exclude student-pilot training accidents, which are the only fair comparison). Twin-engine aircraft don't fly very well on one engine, and when one engine quits, your problems have only begun, because the skill required to deal with the emergency is often beyond that of the businessman/pilot, unless he constantly practices and prepares for engine-out emergencies. And engine failures are most likely at the most critical times—takeoff, for example, when engines are under maximum stress, and a split second of indecision or a small error can kill you.

Our nation has developed a distribution and marketing system of incredible complexity that functions beautifully as long as our economic aircraft is not bounced around too vigorously by financial turbulence. But the chance of malfunction increases as economic stresses and complexities multiply.

The analogy is almost perfect. Consider the miracle of food on the supermarket shelf. Every day shoppers spend tens of millions of dollars in the supermarkets of America, and the next day, as if by magic, those shelves are full again and ready for more hordes of shoppers. How does it happen? It is the end result of a complex system that gets food from the ground into your home.

The process depends on an efficient transportation system (which, in the USA, depends upon profits to reward the trucker) and labor peace. It also depends upon normal credit and a sound banking system so the farmer is willing to deliver his wheat on credit to the elevator operator who delivers it on credit to the barge operator, who takes it down the Mississippi, and so on up the chain, until the supermarket trusts you and the banking system enough to accept your check for a loaf of bread. Imagine what would happen to that system if the banks were in trouble and everyone's ability to pay was in doubt. Would they accept your check at the checkout counter? Would credit be routinely extended at every point in that complex chain?

What if the inflationary spiral triggered labor trouble (as inflation always does) with a gauntlet of picket lines to be crossed by union truck drivers (if they aren't on strike) between the farmer and you at any one of the crucial transfer points on the chain of transactions? Remember the inflation losses faced by lenders under inflation? If the credit system became unworkable, we would have to totally reorganize the system by which people are paid for their products or services, and the changes would be monumental, disruptive, and would take time to correct, perhaps a long time.

What if the rising spiral of inflation, rising interest rates, and a collapsing bond market and deepening recession causes mass unemployment in the cities, forcing cities into bankruptcy by draining the public treasuries, exhausting all the unemployment funds, and causing civil disorders as angry people realize that government promises are going to be broken? Would food move into your local supermarket, and could you safely walk in with your money and walk out with your food?

During the 1974–75 recession, we came within a gnat's eyelash of losing our banking system or, at the very least, having to shut down for awhile. How do you buy food if the banks are closed, or aren't trusted enough for the supermarket to accept your check? The banks will go into the next recession more fragile and vulnerably weaker than the last one.

We will recover, of course, after some pain, but the big question is: Will you get through with your wealth and health intact?

Personal Problems

There is another good reason for having an emergency commodity storage program that does not require a nationwide war, calamity, or famine, and that converted me to this idea.

A cousin of mine from Wyoming was passing through town, looking for work as a carpenter, so my wife and I decided to have him build some shelves for us in the garage so we could have a place for an emergency food-storage program. It's a little embarrassing because the LDS Church has been telling its members for many years to have a storage program, and I didn't have one. But I resolved to repent.

So he built our shelves for us and earned a little money. Kay began to squirrel away some money from the food budget to buy extra food and canned goods. At the time, I was running a speed-reading school franchise, and then trouble hit. I had published an eight-page advertising supplement for the newspapers, aimed at specific events with specific times and specific places. The day before it was to run in all the

Bay area newspapers, a wildcat strike hit the *San Francisco Examiner* and quickly spread to all the other papers. We had a great big pile of newsprint that was no good. It had cost me $25,000, which was about all my operating capital. The strike continued for several months, right at the time of my usual biggest sales period of the year. Over time it eventually led to a bankruptcy, as the parent company canceled my franchise and secretly sold it to one of my employees who had a wealthy family.

I came home that day having gone to work rich (I thought) and came home broke, which ruined my whole day. Kay and I stood in the garage and looked at that stored food. I had my arms around her, and we both had tears. There was no generalized famine or economic trouble in the world, but there was a famine at 27 Arroyo Drive in Moraga, California. That's when I began to realize the wisdom of the counsel we had received from church leaders for many years. That is what formed the basis for this book.

With the troubles I've been suggesting, even if the country hangs together and distribution systems are still working, there will be lots of little tragedies with a lot of people out of work and government unwilling or unable to back them up; thus the wisdom of this chapter.

STORED FOOD

I've talked to hundreds of clients who say, "I agree with your philosophy and I would like to ask you a question," and then they ask me my advice about money. When I routinely check to see if they have a food-storage plan, they say, "Well, no. I haven't done that yet. But I have some silver coins. I'll always be able to buy food with silver coins, even if the currency collapses." But, brother, you can't buy it if it isn't being transported. You can't buy it if there's panic at the supermarkets and there's a crowd standing around waiting to storm the delivery truck.

MY KINGDOM FOR A LOAF OF BREAD

The delivery chain can even be upset by the weather, as indicated by an article from the *Indianapolis Star*, January 30, 1978, during a big snowstorm that hit the MidWest.

> When a Pepperidge Farms delivery truck carrying bread to Fort Benjamin Harrison Saturday night broke down near the Marsh Delicatessen at 62nd Street and Allisonville Road, the store's enterprising assistant manager saw a golden opportunity and negotiated for the bread.
>
> But when some 50 persons shopping at the store realized what was going on, Dan Dudley was almost sorry he had. The shoppers rushed the truck in an every-man-for-himself frenzy to get the bread. "Two men even got into a fist-fight over a loaf," Dudley said. "I didn't think the guy was going to make it into the store alive."

On February 2, also in Indianapolis, another article reported the following:

> Grocery store cash registers continued to ring madly Wednesday and truck delivery men scurried around the city trying to keep up with the demand of customers flocking to stores in fear that a winter-storm watch might develop into a blizzard.
>
> "They're buying everything they can get their hands on,"

the manager of the Kroger store at 4100 South East Street said.

The grocery store rush began Tuesday night after the forecast for more snow was made. Customers evidently were recalling what it was like when they opened their refrigerators and found empty shelves when the worst blizzard in the city's history raged outside last week.

A Kroger manager at 2620 West Michigan Street said persons were buying "ridiculous" amounts of milk, bread and eggs. "We can't keep bread in the store," he added.

The significance of these two stories is that panic buying could occur even if there isn't a real problem, but if people anticipate one.

There are all kinds of other reasons for having an emergency supply of commodities on hand. Let me give you a few.

Back in 1968 when my business went down the tubes, these commodities helped sustain us during the next several months until I could establish a new income and get on my feet. If we had not had it, perhaps we would not have been able to use what money I could earn or borrow to continue to make the payments on our home and maintain some semblance of stability through that very difficult period.

In the next economic downturn, some of you will lose your jobs or find your businesses in trouble. The peace of mind and security that comes from having an emergency commodity supply in a period of vulnerability makes it worthwhile, even if you never have to consume it. Just being able to stay home if there is any kind of civil disruption is important to your personal safety and peace of mind.

As this edition of this book is written, the dollar is sinking into both oceans because we are sending more money abroad for imports than is coming into this country to buy our exports. If the dollar shrinks much further, the international monetary system may come unglued.

With all these pressures, plus continued monetary inflation, prices will continue to soar. A storage program for food and other commodities purchased now will give you an outstanding return on your investment—tax free—as your profit consists of the money you don't spend later to buy expensive things when prices explode. They can't raise prices on things you bought last year.

OIL TO FOOD

The American farming system has become almost entirely dependent upon large-scale application of fertilizers, pesticides, herbicides, and other chemicals made from petroleum and natural gas. It can truly be said that the food chain begins in the sands of Saudi Arabia or in the bowels of the earth below the Gulf Coast of Louisiana. Government policies and controls have locked into place those factors that will create inevitable growing energy shortages. At the present time, we are importing more than 50% of our oil, about half of that from the Persian Gulf and Venezuela. If OPEC or Venezuelan president Hugo Chavez should ever squeeze us again with an oil boycott, we could find our food chain cut off at the first link.

If farmers cannot continue to apply the petroleum-based pesticides and fungicides to protect the Green Revolution plants that were bred for yield, not resistance to insect infestation and disease, and if we cannot run the pumps to irrigate those crops, which were not bred for hardiness or drought-resistance, or if we cannot continue to literally and figuratively pour back into the soil eleven calories of energy, mostly in the form of petroleum or its derivatives, for every calorie of food we take out of it, the nation's food production could be crippled.

Odds

I consider one or more of these problems to be very possible. If I had to identify the most likely threat, it would be the inflation-caused disruption of the nation's marketplace, and that's possible at any time. That brings us back to a previous concept, which is that some of your inflating greenbacks should be exchanged now for those things without which your life would be difficult or uncomfortable if you couldn't buy them anytime you wanted.

Storing, or, as the popular press likes to call it somewhat derisively, "hoarding" food and other goods sounds a bit paranoid to a lot of people, because it implies that there will be a need for it, and most people simply can't make that mental leap. In fact, I would bet that two-thirds of the subscribers to my newsletter who think they have wholeheartedly accepted my opinions of the effect of inflation on their lives, have not been emotionally able to make the logical move of storing food and other commodities, and that is so sad, because it is the one piece of advice in this book in which there is no risk whatsoever. It is an essential part of your financial planning, and if you are not willing to do that, you probably didn't believe the rest of this book. If I'm wrong, the worst thing that would ever happen to you is that you would eat it or use it and save some money.

Modern storage foods are a long cry from the old K-rations. Available dehydrated and freeze-dried foods are almost indistinguishable from the fresh product. There is no waste. What comes out of a can is 100% edible.

You spend hundreds of dollars every year to insure your cars against the accident you fully expect not to have, and you can't eat the canceled checks. Your money is wasted unless you're "lucky" enough to have an accident. Commodity storage is the insurance you can eat. And just to give you one more perspective, if inflation disrupted the system, wouldn't you wish your neighbor had a food storage program?

A discussion of this subject usually raises so many moral and technical questions, I'd like to raise some of these questions and answer them.

Q: Isn't it likely that if I store food and we should have a famine, that hungry people might try to take it away from me and I might have to defend myself with guns?

A: That's silly, and it's based on the following rather shaky assumptions: 1) there will be no food anywhere and hordes of people will cast aside all civilized restraint; and 2) you can outgun a mob. The picture of you sitting on your pile of dehydrated food, holding off a mob of neighbors with guns simply doesn't square with any of the lessons of history. It just doesn't happen that way.

I expect to use my storage program to tide me over brief periods of shortages, and periods where the variety and quality of commodities that I need to maintain normal life may not be available. I can supplement that which is available by dipping into my storage. This is not a preparation for the end of the world. That's impossible. It is a preparation for a period of personal hardship, possible loss of job or failure of your business, temporary disruptions in distribution, and a period of national convalescence when you may not be able to buy what you want, when you want it, in the quantity and quality you want.

Just as a rudimentary caution, I also would not have a neon sign in front of my home that reads FOOD HERE. I would also like my neighbors to have a food storage plan. And I have stored some extra food to help others. The best way I know to persuade them to prepare themselves is to put this book in their hands. It will probably be a better persuader than you, so loan this to them or give them one for their own library.

But back to the hard question. Would I shoot someone if they threatened my life or well-being in a period of lawlessness? Of course I would, and probably so would you. If anyone came to hurt me or take my property by force, I would do whatever was necessary to protect my wife, but I prefer to plan my life so that eventuality is the lowest possible on the probability scale. We should never lose our feelings for the sanctity of human life. The one thing that must survive all these difficulties is the collective values that make nations governable and societies peaceful.

Just to add a note of levity, one of my subscribers told me, "I have a storage program. I'm going to buy a gun and move next door to a Mormon!" Ha, ha! Good luck, because many Mormons, often being enthusiastic outdoorsmen, are hunters and own their own guns.

Q: Is it moral to store commodities when people are doing without? If everyone took your advice, wouldn't it create shortages?

A: There is enough surplus grain now to provide between

100 and 150 pounds for every man, woman, and child in America, and wheat is one of the basics of my food storage program. A massive food storage movement would strengthen food prices.

It is moral to take my advice in times of surplus. If you wait until there are shortages and scramble to grab more than your share of the limited available supply, that's "hoarding," and that's immoral, and the government may even make it illegal by rationing.

When people store things in times of plenty, they will not be competing for things when they are scarce, and there is more for everyone else, including the poor and the profligate. I'm sure that the people in my hometown will be glad not to have me standing in the store line ahead of them with my big family. I won't have to because I will have taken care of myself with my choice of goods at much lower prices, long before the problem occurs.

Q: Where can you store food, and how much space does it take?

A: The concentrated dehydrated-foods commercial storage programs only need approximately one-quarter to one-seventh the space of an equivalent amount of fresh food. If you use the proper mix of grains, beans, rice, supplements, and dehydrated and freeze-dried foods for a balanced and interesting diet, a year's supply for one person could be put under one and a half card tables. That can easily be stored in the bottom two or three feet of your closet. Properly prepared, it requires no specialized storage facilities, and it doesn't take up a lot of room.

Q: How long will it last?

A: Nitrogen-packed dehydrated food has a nutritional shelf life of from four to seven years, which means it will not start losing nutritional value for at least four years, depending on the temperature at which it is stored. Wheat, if kept dry and protected from rodents and insects, will last for two or three thousand years. Some that was found in the tomb of King Tut was still edible, and it even germinated.

Q: How much does a good food storage program cost?

A: If you prepare a complete do-it-yourself program, like many Mormons have done (contact your local LDS ward and ask for the president of the women's organization, the Relief Society; they are very happy to help), you could set aside an austere six-month supply of food for as little as $200. If you want an interesting, varied diet that falls somewhat short of gourmet fare, but by any reasonable measurement is attractive, using some dehydrated and freeze-dried foods, you could obtain a six-month supply for one person for $200 to $400. Price-wise, that is very close to cost of feeding one person for a year, shopping at your local supermarket. In fact, it's a little bit less. The Bureau of Economic Analysis says the average American family is now spending about $950 per month on food, or $11,400 per year.

If you want a real luxurious gourmet food program based entirely on freeze-dried foods, complete with beef stroganoff, shrimp Creole, and sirloin steak, you can pay as much as $1,000 to $2,000 for six months. It all depends on your pocketbook and your inclinations, but in any event, it isn't a heck of a lot, compared with what you are now spending on food. And you can buy your program a bit at a time.

Q: When should I buy this food?

A: You already know the answer to that question. Buy it now! I'd rather be a year too early than a few days too late. Until you have done it, you shouldn't be following any of my other advice. If your money is limited, then do what you can. It's your surest investment from a strictly dollars-and-cents point of view, and it's the one indispensable but riskless piece of advice that applies to everyone. Disruptions in the marketplace can come with stunning swiftness, and labor troubles, terrorism, gas rationing—any number of things—could create problems overnight. You might not need it for a year or two, or five. But then again, you might need it tomorrow.

Nuts and Bolts

I hope I've made my point as to why you need an emergency supply. If I haven't persuaded you, you might as well skip the rest of this chapter because I'm now going to tell you how to do it. You need a carefully reasoned advance response to the potential problems that make good sense for these times—an insurance policy against hunger and inconvenience. You can't get insurance when the barn's on fire. The best insurance is to become self-sufficient.

There are three basic ways to do it.

1. Nineteenth-century style. If you live on a farm or have an acre or two, you can become self-sufficient by using intensive methods of organic gardening and by raising chickens and rabbits. You would then have relatively little need for a food storage plan, although you might want to have some commercially prepared foodstuffs set aside for the winter and spring when supplies might run low, or as a protection against crop failure. If there is good hunting or fishing nearby, so much the better. If you have the land, the skills, and the inclination, that's a great way to go.

2. **A do-it-yourself food storage plan**—the approach that has been adopted by many Mormons. Most of you can't be self-sufficient in food production, although most everyone can grow something, even if it's only in a window box or a sprouter. You buy certain bulk basics, such as wheat, powdered milk, honey, salt, beans, etc., and you can purchase containers and prepare them for long-term storage. This approach to do-it-yourself storage is a lot of work, but it can be a real money saver.

There are several outstanding books on this subject that have treated it far better than I can in these pages, which you should add to your library. *Making the Best of Basics* by James Talmage Stevens, and *Passport to Survival* by Esther Dickey are classics.

3. **The commercial dehydrated or freeze-dried food storage plan.** These programs are prepared by firms that are in the business of preparing food storage. They consist primarily of dehydrated and freeze-dried foods with some grains and food supplements. They range in price from $2,000 or more for a six-month supply of luxurious gourmet freeze-dried meals, which are indistinguishable from that which you would consume in a middle-quality restaurant, on down to somewhat less spectacular programs, which offer good variety and taste

in the $500 to $1,000 range. There is a tremendous variety for your pocketbook and palate. The problem is that most of these programs have some serious nutritional problems.

Back in 1973, when I became concerned about the state of the nation and began thinking through the implications for my family, my instinctive response was to look at the commercial food storage programs, because I am not a farmer, nor do I have time to do a heck of a lot of do-it-yourself stuff. I have a deep interest in health and nutrition, and I was in the food supplement business at that time. I am an obsessive reader of nutritional literature, ranging from the far-out natural food freaks to the mainstream scientific and professional journals, so I felt reasonably qualified to choose a sound program.

I found to my horror that the commercial plans I looked at were totally at odds with the healthy nutrition lifestyle I had chosen for myself and my family. There wasn't one that I would buy as a "unit," which was the way they were being sold. I would have to design my own unit. When I began delving into the food storage industry, I found that not only were many of the programs nutritionally unsound, but most of the companies were unstable. One of the largest had just gone broke, and there were lengthy delays in delivery—as much as six months. It was a growth industry undergoing a typical shakeout.

The food storage business is literally "feast or famine." When people are scared and we're sliding into a recession, the companies can't meet the demand. They then expand capacity, and just about the time they are ready to handle the increased volume, the panic is over, business falls off to zilch, and they find themselves in financial trouble. They are victims of a wildly swinging business cycle.

Let's look at the dos and don'ts of food storage.

First, the don'ts:

1. Don't rush out and buy a lot of canned and frozen goods. They both have problems for storage.

The most significant measurement of the quantity of food is the calorie, which is a measurement of the amount of food energy that will be derived from it. Canned goods are expensive, relative to the "cost-per-calorie." Canned goods consist of part water and part product. Not only is it expensive to ship water back and forth across the country, but the taste and color is generally inferior to the dehydrated or frozen product, particularly in vegetables.

The shelf life of canned goods is somewhat in doubt, despite the protestations of the industry. I published in my newsletter a study from the University of Idaho Agricultural Extension Service by Don Huber, plant pathologist, and Esther H. Wilson, extension nutrition specialist, entitled "Store a Year's Supply of Food and Household Items." It triggered a rather irate letter from an old friend who was a Washington lobbyist for the canning industry, but I have not yet seen a refutation of the data. What interested me most were the tables on the shelf life of foods.

Not only is the nutritional value of canned goods lower because of the heat used in canning, but the "nutritional shelf life" is brief at best. By "nutritional shelf life" I mean the length of time you can count on the food having the same value that it had when it was canned. The nutritional value deteriorates long before the food begins to deteriorate enough to become unpalatable or dangerous.

STORAGE LIFE OF CANNED GOODS

Canned Goods	Storage Life
DAIRY PRODUCTS	
Powdered Milk	1 year
MEAT PRODUCTS	
Beef	18 months
Chicken	18 months
Fish (tuna)	1 year
Ham	18 months
Lunch Meat	18 months
Pork	18 months
Turkey	18 months
CANNED VEGETABLES	
All	18 months
FRUITS	
Applesauce	12–18 months
Apricots	12–18 months
Berries	6 months
Citrus Juice	6–8 months
Citrus Slices	12–18 months
Cherries	6–12 months
Peaches	12–18 months
Pears	12–18 months
Pineapple	12–18 months
Plums	12–18 months
MISCELLANEOUS	
Peanut Butter	12–18 months
Shelled Nuts	1 year

If you store some canned goods, rotate them, use them regularly, and replace them well within the storage-life figures from the above table. Also, you need to compensate for the nutritional losses with a good natural multivitamin supplement and extra vitamin C.

Don't use any cans that are bulging, leaking, or rusted. "If in doubt, throw it out."

Frozen food has an even shorter shelf life, to say nothing of the vulnerability to power outages, and in a period of real financial or economic chaos, I would not want to have to depend upon a steady flow of electricity to your home. If you do store frozen food, make sure you have a smoker unit so that any meat or fish could have its shelf life extended by smoking if the power went out for long. Canned and frozen foods can be part of a short-term storage program, but for long-term storage there are much better alternatives. If my forecasts are right over the long haul, but my timetable is off by a year or two, you want to be sure you can safely eat your stored food with good nutritional results some years after its acquisition.

2. Don't just buy any "food unit" from any food storage dealer without following the guidelines in this chapter. Many of the "units" are based on economic considerations rather than sound nutritional principles, and even those companies that have made an effort to be nutritionally sound have generally relied upon government nutritional tables, which have very little relevance to reality. I haven't seen anything yet the government has not been able to foul up. And in my opinion, the Food and Drug Administration is the most biased, industry-influenced regulatory agency of all, and I would not depend on any data produced by the FDA. They are captives

of the food processing and sugar industries, and that bias is reflected in their conclusions, their studies, and their press releases.

3. Be very wary of "bargains." Whenever you see a food storage company clearing out a lot of inventory at a cheap price, it is probably reaching the end of its shelf life, or the company is suffering from slow sales and cash difficulties, which means the food may have been sitting around for a long time. It is not likely to be fresh. Shelf life is one of your most important considerations. "Shelf life" means how long it will be of high nutritional value and edibility from the time you buy it, not from the time it was canned. I know of some companies that have had storage food sitting around for more than two years, still for sale. If you see such a bargain, demand documentation on when it was canned. Each can must be coded.

4. Don't just let your food sit there. Rotate it. By that I mean use it and replace it on a regular basis. There are several good reasons for this.

First, it will have a higher nutritional value when you use it if you are constantly replacing it with fresher products, and, second, if the time should ever come that you should need to rely on it for your family, the transition will go a lot smoother if you are accustomed to it. A change of diet to unfamiliar foods can be stressful. If our family had to switch to our emergency storage program, it would take relatively little change in our eating habits (whole or cracked wheat as cereal, or ground wheat as flour for bread). Get used to using whole wheat, beans, protein powders, and the like. It's a healthy diet, and you will also find it a fine way to save money, as foods bought in bulk are a lot cheaper than those bought every week at your supermarket.

5. Don't accept exaggerated shelf life claims of storage foods. A lot of sincere, enthusiastic food storage dealers are claiming that their product will be good for 15 to 20 years. Don't you believe it! I know of too many people who have had to throw out food storage programs after seven to ten years, and I've got a good group to sample in my Mormon friends.

Shelf life has to be measured in two ways. Our first concern is nutritional shelf life, which is the length of time over which you can count on the food having the same nutritional value that it had when it was packaged, particularly in reference to the volatile or water-soluble vitamins (the B-complex and C) and many of the minerals, which will gradually oxidize and break down. The shelf life for most properly packed dehydrated or freeze-dried foods is four to seven years, depending on temperature. The lower the temperature at which the food is stored, the longer the shelf life. There might be a loss in color and flavor after seven years.

6. Don't pay for the food before it is delivered, unless you know the firm and can depend on them. Too many people have paid for food and not had it delivered because of the financial instability of the industry. You can count on our recommended firms, as we monitor their finances and their business on a regular basis, and they are all dependable. The best way to handle it is either to order COD, or to pay a deposit with the order and the balance upon delivery. A legitimate food storage dealer who doesn't know you might object to this, as he will have just as much concern about your ability

and willingness to pay as you would have about his willingness to fulfill the order. The resolution of the stalemate is to know your dealer and trust him if he is dependable.

Now let's discuss some of the dos.

1. Buy a six-month supply of food. I'm not sure six months is enough, but it certainly isn't too much, not because I think the nation would be without food for a half year, but because there is a distinct possibility of intermittent disruption of the marketplace—possibly days or weeks at a time—over several years. It doesn't take very long to get hungry. I would also be able to draw from my emergency food supplies over a period of several years of shortages to replace those foods that may not be available in the quantity, quality, or variety of choices to which I am accustomed. I also feel I should have enough to share with those I love who do not believe my message. I also want some available for barter, so a six-month supply for each member of your family makes pretty good sense

You will obviously have to work within your own financial limitations, but food is your number one priority and comes ahead of any of my investment recommendations. I wouldn't want to be the richest hungry man on my block.

2. Be sure your program is nutritionally sound. Nutrition may bore some of you, but if you don't want to take the trouble to plow through this nutritional stuff, maybe there is someone in your family who will, so delegate that responsibility. Your choice is to either take my advice about our recommended dealers and trust them to sell you what you should have, or get an education on the subject through this chapter.

Here are the fundamentals of nutrition as it relates to emergency storage:

Think of your emergency storage program as though it were a target. The most points are in the bull's-eye, and you receive lesser points as you move to the outside of the target. The ideal food storage program will be arranged in that manner.

In the bull's-eye I have put food supplements. If you have met all of your nutritional requirements for the elements that your body is known to need, you could probably live on edible weeds and roots if you had to. (There are several good books on that subject available in paperback, including *Field Guide to Edible Wild Plants* by Bradford Angier.) After your nutritional requirements are assured from supplements, the quality of the rest of the food storage program, although still very important, is not as critical. You can gain sufficient bulk and calories from almost anything.

This is exactly the reverse of what your present eating habits should be. You are generally better off getting all of your nutrients from the food you eat, if possible, and using supplements for just that—supplementation, which Kay and I do routinely. In an emergency situation, your problem is exactly reversed. Even the best of food storage programs come up short nutritionally, because your nutritional needs increase under stress, and obviously we are talking about a time of potential great stress. Also, the processing of foods for long-term storage, under the best of conditions, will result in some nutritional losses, plus the aforementioned losses under storage.

You cannot afford to get sick. Many critical medications, such as penicillin, depend on petrochemicals in their manufacturing process. Staying well becomes a matter of something more than convenience. Sickness that is now routinely handled by a trip to the doctor for a shot could become life-threatening. In addition, there might not be the fuel for you to get to a doctor, and the doctor might not have all of the high-technology electric and chemical tools at his disposal to help you. Your best bet is to stay well, and the greater the stress, the more difficult that is.

A technical bulletin used by California Vegetable Concentrates (CVC), a division of General Foods that makes dehydrated foods for the storage food industry, is very candid about it. "There is no truly reliable representative nutritional information pertaining to commercially processed dehydrated vegetables. What work has been done on processed vegetables has been fragmentary, difficult to correlate for many reasons, and of only indicative value in determining food values.

" . . . values shown for dehydrated vegetables have been calculated based on concentration ratios with no assumed processing losses." That means that nutritional tables for dried foods are an approximation, at best, based on government tables of food values that assume the product is fresh. CVC says further: "We know of no data indicating retention of nutritional values after prolonged storage. CVC vegetables do retain good color and flavor for periods in excess of one year and in several instances, for considerably longer periods when held at 70 degrees F. or below." The answer to that uncertainty is simple. Store food supplements, to be sure that you are consuming sufficient nutrients to compensate for that great unknown.

Another reason for supplementation is that, in the interests of processing difficulties, or shelf life considerations, a lot of foods you are accustomed to are not included in storage programs. Fresh meat, eggs, fish, and dairy products, which presently provide most of your protein and much of your vitamins A and B, are either missing, in short supply, overprocessed, or terribly expensive in most food storage programs. The major protein substitutes (beans, rice, etc.) are both lower protein percentage and much lower protein quality, although that level can be improved somewhat when different foods are consumed in the same meal (wheat and beans, beans and rice, corn and rice).

For a discussion of how to improve the protein value of vegetable proteins, I heartily recommend the book *Diet for a Small Planet* by Frances Moore Lappe. She points out how, for example, you can combine wheat or bread (low in lysine, an essential amino acid) with rice (high in lysine) to improve the protein quality of both foods. That doesn't solve the whole problem, however, as I still believe you need some of the higher-quality animal proteins under stress conditions, but it sure can help.

Stress is not just emotional or mental trauma. Stress can be measured by the degree and rapidity of change in your life. According to those who study stress, even a vacation, Christmas, or a change of diet can trigger the body's stress responses. Under stress, your body produces additional adrenal hormones, which bring about great changes in the body. This is generally some level of response to the "fight or flight" syndrome. God created us so that when stress occurs, the body marshals all of its resources to either fight or run. The severest stress is the death of a spouse or a child. Next to it is a divorce. Even a promotion or change of job is stressful. The problems described in this book are stressful.

When you react to stress this way, you cannibalize your muscle and bone tissues to get high-quality protein to use as raw components for hormones, enzymes, antibodies, white blood cells, and other chemicals. This internal cannibalism makes you more susceptible to disease. In children it can stunt both physical growth and the growth of brain tissue. Under stress conditions you may have a need for well-balanced animal protein, and your body consumes large amounts of vitamin C and the B complex as well as minerals such as calcium. One researcher has indicated that a half hour of severe stress or fear can deplete all of the vitamin C in your blood, and a day of intense worry can destroy all of the vitamin C stored in your adrenal cortex. As vitamin C is a vital component of white blood cells and is a potent viruscide, your resistance to virus and bacterial infections is reduced. Under severe stress conditions, the recommended daily allowance of vitamin C published by the FDA is woefully inadequate, to say nothing of the fact that vitamin C is the most vulnerable of all the vitamins to food-processing losses.

PROTEIN SUPPLEMENTS

Bear in mind that a high-quality protein supplement is merely a concentrated food that in our food storage program is designed to replace those high-quality proteins that are generally omitted because of expense or other factors.

It is also designed to supplement the low-quality vegetable proteins, when consumed in the same meal. For example, if one protein food is high in lysine, a "limiting" amino acid, and another is low in lysine, all your body knows, if you ate them in the same meal at the same time, is that your protein intake is sufficient in lysine. If any of the eight essential amino acids are missing or in short supply, the body's use of it is limited, and your ability to fight infection or rebuild tissue is impaired.

Your protein powder should have the following characteristics:

1. It should taste good. Some protein powders would gag a maggot.

2. It should be rich in lysine and tryptophan; in fact, its lysine level should exceed the ideal amino acid profile of the World Health Organization so that there is extra lysine available in the product to complement the amino-acid profile of the protein in the grains in your storage program. Thus when grains and the right protein supplement are eaten in the same meal, the protein quality of the grain is richly enhanced.

3. Don't pay for protein powder that lists milk powder as one of the first two ingredients. If that's what you want, you can buy milk powder a lot cheaper without paying health food store prices for it.

VITAMINS AND MINERALS

There are probably few subjects on which there is more violent scientific controversy than vitamins and minerals. At issue is whether we need them in supplemental form at all, as well as what form is best. I'd better admit to some bias right here so you can decide whether or not to take my advice. I am convinced that natural vitamins are superior. I would like to expand a little effort making that case. The FDA says that anyone who claims there's any difference between natural and synthetic vitamins is a "quack." That makes me a mallard.

Here's why I disagree.

Chromatography is an analysis method used to literally

photograph molecules of both organic and inorganic substances. Chromatographs show a distinct difference between the synthetic and natural vitamin C molecule. Synthetic ascorbic acid and natural vitamin C are chemically identical, except that the chromatographs of the natural vitamins show "impurities" that have been determined to be enzymes—protein factors that apparently assist the absorption and utilization of the vitamin on a cellular level. The visual difference between the natural and synthetic of these two is dramatic. That doesn't necessarily prove that natural is better than synthetic, but it certainly does prove they are different, and I believe natural is better.

Writing in the August 27, 1973, issue of the *Journal of the American Medical Association*, Dr. Samuel Ayers Jr., an MD from Los Angeles, disputed a contention of Marguerita Magy, MS, of the AMA Department of Foods and Nutrition. She had made the statement (*Journal of the American Medical Association*, July 2, 1973) that biochemically, a vitamin has a single molecular structure, and it doesn't make any difference if it is natural or synthetic because the body can't tell the difference. "That may be true of some vitamins," Dr. Ayers wrote, "but it is definitely not true of Vitamin E (tocopheryl), in which the alpha fraction contains virtually all the therapeutically active principle. D-Alpha-Tocopheryl acetate is derived from natural sources, such as wheat germ oil, whereas dl-Alpha-Tocopheryl acetate is the synthetic form. "While they may appear identical chemically, they affect polarized light differently and in animal experiments the d or natural form is considerably more active than the dl, or synthetic form."

Dr. Ayers cited several sources, who said that the relative potency of d-alpha tocopheryl acetate is 1.2 times (20%)

greater than the dl form (*Nutritional Review*, 24:33–34, 1967). "In order to obtain the maximum therapeutic effect from Vitamin E," Dr. Ayers concluded, "the physician should specify d-alpha-tocopheryl acetate."

British researcher Isabel W. Jennings of the University College of the University of Cambridge speaks of the comparison between synthetic and natural vitamins in her book *Vitamins in Endocrine Metabolism* (Charles C. Thomas, 1970). "The close relations, although useful in many ways, pose some problems in that they may have only a fraction, whether large or small, of the biological activity of the natural product." She points out that while vitamin C, for example, is chemically identical to the natural vitamin and an equally effective antioxidant, it does not have the same value in promoting the health of the capillaries.

For all of these reasons and more, I prefer the natural form of the vitamins.

Natural vitamins generally are more expensive than the synthetic, but they are worth it because of their increased potency. Besides, one or two years into using your stored food is no time to find out that your diet has been lacking in some undiscovered essential nutrient and, as I said before, those nutrients will tend to be associated with natural vitamins as "naturally occurring factors."

Wheat is an ideal storage food because it keeps forever and is one of the most versatile and best-balanced foods found in nature. It only needs to be kept safe from moisture, rodents, and insects. You can buy it in bulk at your local feed store, or you can buy it already canned in one-gallon tins from your food storage dealer. It's a lot cheaper to buy it in bulk; however, it does need to be treated. This is best done by adding some dry ice to the container of wheat, putting the lid on loosely until all the dry ice has dissipated, forming gaseous carbon dioxide, which, being heavier than air, will stay in the container. Then seal the container. If you seal it too early, the buildup of pressure could give you a bad case of wheat shrapnel. Carbon dioxide prevents the development of any weevil eggs that might be in the wheat. It could be kind of disturbing to open up your can of wheat in the middle of a famine and find it seething with little weevil worms, even if weevils are high in protein. That has happened to us, so you need to be very careful. The one-gallon sealed cans of wheat bought from your storage dealer are a lot safer, but cost more. But wheat is still pretty cheap anyway. Our personal storage program wheat is about half bulk and half canned.

Your local Mormon church may have a co-op buying arrangement, which it is happy to share with non-Mormon friends, which would enable you to buy wheat in bulk. It should be very low in moisture, and of the hard red winter wheat variety. It can be ground into flour for various bakery products. It can be cracked and used as a delicious hot cereal, or it can be soaked in water and sprouted and prepared without any cooking whatsoever. It doesn't take a lot of getting used to. The best books on how to use wheat are *Making the Best of Basics*, and Esther Dickey's book *Passport to Survival*.

I have also included beans because they are a complementary protein to wheat, and they should be eaten in the same meal. A piece of 100% whole-wheat bread and a pot of chili give you fairly good protein quality (especially when accompanied by a glass of your favorite protein drink). They both also provide some high-quality carbohydrate, some essential fatty acids, and a fairly good spectrum of B-complex vitamins.

It obviously would be a good idea to have a mill that could be used to grind wheat. We have one that works either by hand or electricity. They are generally in the $150 to $250 range.

Sprouting seeds are not for the purpose of growing a garden but for growing edible sprouts in your kitchen. When sprouted seeds are served in salads or casseroles, the nutritional value is enhanced. It's another method of preparing food without having to cook if you have a real energy shortage. Next you can add dehydrated or freeze-dried vegetables and fruits, along with some soybean-meat analogues (imitations) called TVP, and various condiments and seasonings.

This is where the pitfalls arise in storage programs. This is where most of the commercial food storage programs begin and end. Dehydrated food can be a major source of calories, bulk, and variety. You could live in fairly good health, but it is important for children especially to have enough variety in the diet that their food is palatable to them and they will eat it. Some children have actually starved to death in famines because they would not eat unfamiliar food. Although we are not contemplating that kind of famine, the principle is still valid.

Hydrogenated vegetable oil may be the most dangerous part of the product. Liquid fats (vegetable oils) are highly unsaturated with the exception of coconut oil and olive oil. Polyunsaturated oils are generally thought by cardiologists and nutritionists to lower cholesterol and triglyceride levels in the blood. When a food processor wishes to harden a polyunsaturated oil to get a different consistency (such as making margarine out of corn oil or safflower oil), or to prolong its shelf life, he "hydrogenates" it. It is heated under pressure, and hydrogen is bubbled through it in the presence of a metal catalyst (nickel or platinum). The hydrogen atoms combine with the carbon atoms and the product becomes "saturated" and hardens.

Dr. Bicknell describes it as follows: "The abnormal fatty acids produced by 'hardening' (hydrogenation) are the real worry. The atoms of the molecule of an essential fatty acid (EFA) are arranged in space in a particular manner . . . but hardening may produce a different spatial arrangement, so that a completely abnormal . . . essential fatty acid is produced. The same mistakes are made by the body when presented . . . (with the abnormal EFA). Not only does it fail to benefit by them, but it is deluded by their similarity to normal EFA and so attempts to use them. It starts incorporating them in biochemical reactions and then finds they are the wrong shape: but the reaction has gone too far to jettison them and begin again with normal EFA, so they are not only useless but actually prevent the use of normal EFA. They are in fact anti-EFA. They accentuate in man and animals a deficiency of EFA. An analogy is jamming the wrong key in the lock: not only is the lock not turned, but the right key also is rendered valueless." (Franklin Bicknell, MD, *Chemicals in Food and Farm Produce: Their Harmful Effects* [London: Faber and Faber, 1960], pp. 69–70).

HONEY

Honey in five-gallon containers belongs in your food storage plan in place of sugar. It has a lot of advantages. Common table sugar (sucrose) is a compound sugar consisting of approximately 50% glucose and 50% fructose. Fructose is at least twice as sweet as sucrose and provides most of the sweetness of common table sugar. The sugars found in honey have a much higher ratio of fructose. Consequently, you can do the same sweetening job with less sugar intake, and that's beneficial. Honey is not basically a food, but a relatively healthful condiment.

Honey contains traces of minerals and B vitamins that are used in its metabolism, eliminating much of the "negative nutrient" aspect that plagues sugar. Once you and your family have used it for a little while, you will probably prefer its taste over that of sugar. It is the major sweetener we use in our home, along with stevia, an herbal sweetener available at any health food store.

Honey keeps virtually forever. For reasons I don't understand, bacteria cannot exist in honey. It does crystallize and become solid, however, but this is readily solved by putting the container in a large pot of water and heating it until the honey liquefies. In the summer you can get the same job done just by putting the container in the sun for a couple of days.

We like to transfer a five-gallon container of honey into smaller containers, as a thirty-pound can is pretty hard to handle when it has gone solid and you are trying to pour it.

SUMMING UP

To sum up my advice on food storage:

1. Store a six-month supply of food and other commodities which, if they were unavailable, would make your life difficult or unpleasant.

2. Make sure it's nutritionally balanced as an antistress program.

3. Don't rely solely on canned or frozen foods.

4. Rotate your food supply and replace as needed.

5. Don't buy a "junk food" storage program. Your health requires that you eat soundly, as you don't dare become ill in the uncertain world ahead of us.

6. Buy it now. Transportation problems can come with stunning suddenness, and the food distribution chain is most vulnerable to labor problems. If you acted today, it would possibly be a few weeks before a commercial food-storage program was delivered. It wasn't raining when Noah built the ark. Buy your food before it becomes "hoarding," at a time when it is readily and freely available and the marketplace is functioning properly.

Frequently Asked Emergency
Storage Questions

Q: Which is better, freeze-dried or dehydrated food?

A: Dehydrated food is generally less expensive and occupies less space. It also takes longer to reconstitute, generally requiring more water and some cooking or overnight soaking. There are no commercially available dehydrated meats, eggs, fish, or fowl. Dehydrated food is the cheapest way to build a very palatable, acceptable food storage program.

Freeze-dried food offers more variety, and freeze-dried meats, shrimp, tuna, eggs, etc., are very acceptable, although quite expensive. A freeze-dried storage program will be considerably more expensive than a dehydrated program, but the ease of reconstitution makes it very attractive. To reconstitute freeze-dried shrimp, all you have to do is soak it in water just a few minutes. Freeze-dried casseroles and combination dishes are ready to eat when mixed for sixty seconds or so in boiling water. The elegant combination dishes, however, such as shrimp Creole, beef stroganoff, and so on are loaded with chemical additives and flavor enhancers.

A well-balanced, inexpensive food storage program will consist of supplements, grains, and dehydrated foods with some freeze-dried products. Then you add a few luxury items such as freeze-dried meat, fish, and combination casserole dishes as "reward foods."

As for taste, I give a slight edge to freeze-dried food, but not much.

Q: What if someone is allergic to wheat and milk? They are the most common food allergies.

A: It makes your problem a little more difficult, but not impossible. You can buy dried corn, cornmeal, oats, and rice. They don't have the long-term storage capabilities of wheat, but can be stored for up to three years.

Q: Are there ways to prepare your own dehydrated food?

A: You bet there are. There are several excellent dehydrators on the market. You buy fruits, vegetables, in fact, almost any food product—and slice it thin, dip the slices in an ascorbic acid (vitamin C) solution or diluted lemon juice, and dry them for twenty-four hours or so. There are several good books on the subject, the best of which are *The ABC's of Home Food Dehydration* by Barbara Densley, and *Home Food Dehydration* by Emme Wheeler.

Q: How much food do I really need for six months?

A: The calorie count is a determining factor. The average person could safely rely on the following table.

AVERAGE CALORIES REQUIRED DAILY

(Depending on size and physical activity)

Adult Male	2000–3500
Adult Female	1800–2500
Teenagers	2000–3000
Children under 12	1000–2000

I figure that if the storage program averages 2000 to 2500 calories a day that it will average out reasonably well over a family, with the small children needing less and a hardworking father needing more.

Nonfood Commodities

We can't store everything in the world, but we can look about us and determine those miscellaneous items that are crucial to your comfort and well-being and your ability to function in a disrupted society. There are several miscellaneous items that should be included in your storage program if you are going to realistically prepare for possible hard times. At the risk of being repetitious, let me remind you that when inflation rages past the 20% level, the marketplace is in danger of being disrupted and a lot of things you take for granted may not be there to buy, or will be priced out of sight. I have a few fundamental recommendations.

ENERGY SELF-SUFFICIENCY

There are so many ways that our gas and electricity and heating oil supplies can be cut off that I think it is simple prudence in a cold climate to have a wood- or charcoal-burning grill, and a supply of charcoal, or you can have a good gas grill and a substantial supply of propane. (Don't use them indoors; that's dangerous!)

There are heating units that can be installed in your existing fireplace to minimize heat loss. Most people don't realize that you can't heat a house with a fireplace. It generally creates a negative flow of warm air. When the fire is lit, the hot air rises up the chimney, drawing air out of the room. Cold air is drawn into the house through cracks and openings, and the net effect is that the rooms away from the immediate vicinity of the fireplace get colder. There is more heat lost up the chimney than is gained through radiation into the room. However, attachments can be installed in your fireplace that will recirculate hot air back into the home and actually heat a really good-sized home with a properly equipped fireplace. There are several good ones available on the market.

WATER STORAGE

If you are storing dehydrated food, it takes a lot of water to reconstitute and prepare it. There are any number of things that could disrupt your water supply. If the pumping stations were put out of action by terrorists, or simply a major power failure, you could have problems. During the New York City blackout, most buildings were not able to get water from faucets above the third or fourth floor. If this happens for just a few hours, it's a minor inconvenience with a little discomfort, but if it lasts more than a day in the hot summer, it could be a serious problem. Emergency water storage is another of those harmless ideas that cost you nothing but could be lifesaving.

You should store at least two weeks of cooking and drinking water, more if possible.

ODDS AND ENDS

Go through your house, room by room, drawer by drawer, cupboard by cupboard, and take a look at all of the items that would make life difficult or uncomfortable if you couldn't buy them on a regular recurring basis, and stockpile them.

When you would ordinarily buy one, buy three. Buy spare parts for your car, such as fan belts, hoses, points, plugs, and the like. A few spare tires on hand wouldn't hurt. It will be an excellent investment as they are going to cost a great deal more in the future. If you have small children, don't forget diapers, possibly old-fashioned cloth diapers. And don't forget toilet paper, baby wipes, and paper tissue.

TRANSPORTATION SELF-SUFFICIENCY

Have a fuel-efficient car (fully gassed at all times), and maybe a bike or a moped.

FISHING AND HUNTING

I'm so often asked if you should store guns. No, I don't think you should store guns. You should use guns. Anyone who wants to be self-sufficient should become a reasonably effective hunter. I have never hunted before, being a fisherman by inclination and temperament, but I will be out during the appropriate seasons, as I think it will be important to the supplementation of my diet. Also, it doesn't hurt to have the security of knowing that I can protect my family if necessary, even though I consider that necessity a low probability in my neighborhood. I doubt if there will be a better barter item in a period of currency breakdown than standard ammo, and it may be the best possible investment you could make, not just for barter purposes, but for price appreciation in an inflating monetary system.

MEDICATIONS

If you have a medical problem, consult your doctor and stock plenty of the appropriate medication and check the literature or consult with the manufacturer about the shelf life so you can rotate it at appropriate intervals.

POWER

I would also keep plenty of batteries of all sizes, preferably the rechargeable kind, with a battery charger. After charging them fully, keep them in the refrigerator as the charge will hold almost forever if they are kept cold. A transistor radio to keep you abreast of events, even in the case of power failure, is essential.

I would stock lots of paper goods, including plates, napkins, paper towels, cups, and of course, toilet paper, plus soap and candles.

A complete tool kit and carpentry kit for small repairs would be one great investment. Learn to use them. Buy any one of several excellent manuals on home and automobile repairs and get acquainted with them. A self-sufficient "jack-of-all-trades" will be king in a shortage economy, and anything you can do to educate yourself along these lines can only be helpful.

Much of the information I have given you is just common sense, and you didn't really need to get it from me. Now that I've jogged your thinking, sit down and make a list after you have gone through the house, and I'm sure you will be able to add a lot of items to the list. Some of the items are readily available in local stores, and some can be bought from the sources listed at the end of the book.

An Emergency Survival Kit

Katrina and other natural disasters have taught some tough lessons. Natural disasters could be a lot less stressful if each member of our family has an emergency survival kit (72-hour kit) filled with essentials for survival. Disasters happen anytime and anywhere. Water, electricity, and telephones could be out for days. Cell phones might work, but they might not. Here in Utah, we are due for a major earthquake; it isn't a matter of "if" but "when."

There usually isn't much time to respond. In 2007 there was a summer full of fires in the West and floods in the Midwest, making home evacuations necessary. When disaster happens, local officials and relief workers will get there as soon as they can, but it might not be immediate—it could take hours or even days. Imagine how the Katrina disaster would have changed if even a quarter of the people had an emergency survival kit in hand.

Several websites give good information about preparing emergency kits; www.ready.gov and www.redcross.org are excellent. You should have one for each member of your family. If you don't want to gather the supplies yourself, some companies are happy to sell you prepared kits; www.beprepared.com and www.preparednessplus.net are good ones.

Even if you buy ready-made kits, take time and think through what your family needs individually for three or four days and personalize them. Does someone need daily medication? You will need extra clothes—go through each kit in the spring and fall so you have proper clothing for the season. Kids grow fast, so be sure to have the right sizes.

Make sure you have the basics: water, food, first-aid supplies, necessary medicines, tools and supplies, sanitation needs, bedding, maybe even a game that your family likes to play together—a deck of cards doesn't take up much space.

An emergency kit should be assembled before a disaster strikes. Once disaster hits, the time is past for gathering supplies. But if you've gathered supplies in advance, your family is ready for an evacuation or home confinement.

ACTION STEPS

Do an Internet search of "emergency kits" or "72-hour kits" on your computer. Do it now; you never know when it will be your turn to survive a disaster or run from a forest fire or an earthquake.

The website www.beprepared.com/ruff is a good site for information and supplies. Be sure to use the "/ruff" to get a special Ruff discount. Emergency Essentials is based in Utah and has a good history. You can buy everything there for your emergency kit to a full year's supply of food. You can call them at 800-999-1863.

We have also arranged a special discount with Preparedness Plus. They deal direct with a warehouse, so the food will be fresher. They can also help with special food allergies. The website is www.preparednessplus.net. Enter "Howard Ruff" on the coupon-redemption code at check out for the special discount. Call them at 800-588-5412.

I worked with Norvel Martens for years with Neolife. They have a great food-storage program I helped to design. They are not the cheapest, but they are reliable. Visit their website at www.martensurvival.com or call them at 800-824-7861.

Karen Varner has worked with my subscribers for a number of years. You can email her at your72hrkitlady@yahoo.com or you can call her at 801-225-0948 (it's not toll-free). Please do your homework before you contact Karen. She has coordinated the group discounts, and unless you have something unique, you should be able to buy what you need at the websites above. If you have specific needs like allergies or bulk-bucket discounts don't hesitate to pick her brain.

PART 3

TRUE WEALTH: GOLD OUT OF STRAW

In part I, I covered the economics behind major fiscal problems America faces. In part II, I discussed how you and your family can protect yourself from those difficulties with strategies that are fundamental to preserving live, limb, and homestead during a period of social and financial dislocation. Now in part III, it's time to talk about prosperity and what to do with the money you have left over. Many of my part II survival recommendations will also be good moneymaking strategies in the environment that I foresee. For example, your gold and silver coins would do very well in a relatively orderly inflationary world, as well as in a chaotic coming-down-around-your-ears financial and social collapse. In part III, I may use the same investments for conservative breakthrough approaches and more aggressive, somewhat speculative, high-odds-win-the-game-big strategies involving somewhat higher risks, along with much greater potential rewards.

The investment recommendations in this section are for you to hang on to as long as the very long-term broad trends are inflationary, while ignoring the possible short-term and intermediate (up to three years and) corrections in the trends. If, however, I am wrong about the severity of the inflationary spiral, you have to be ready to catch the economy going both ways. If you should have a recovery from inflation, but terrorism is still a danger, you would still hang on to your survival silver and gold coins, your food storage plan, etc., because they are your chaos insurance. But if you have any funds left over after taking my survival advice, you can adopt a much more flexible strategy with those funds to prosper and even get rich from the trends. That's what part III is all about.

Section III is the climax of the book. I hope the rest of the book has laid a foundation for these strategies. Don't short-cut past the survival steps. If you contact me for advice on how to implement the strategies in part III, and had not taken the basic steps in part II, I wouldn't be very interested in talking to you, because it could be dangerous—financially and personally.

8

GOLD AND SILVER: WHEN, WHERE, WHY, AND HOW

There are a lot of dumb things you can do with your money in 2007–8, but *not* buying gold or silver will cost you more money than all of them put together. There are a lot of reasons why this is so, but a few of them stand out—like these:

1. Gold and silver are early in historic bull markets (in fact, as this is written, it's only a "golden calf"), making this a low-risk investment with an awesome upside for the long-term investor.

2. This bull market will dwarf the last great one in 1973–81, when fortunes were made by relatively small amounts of money invested by amateur investors (many of them my readers).

3. All of the factors that created the last bull market are here again, only several times greater, not the least of which is far more money creation than in the seventies.

4. Rising gold and silver jewelry demand by the hundreds of millions of brand-new middle-class workers in India and China is now an indigestible fact of life. Silver, the real monetary metal, is now also a critical industrial metal with thousands of irreplaceable applications; the needs of industry can no longer be met from existing supplies (see chapter 10). Demand by investors, industry, and jewelry fabricators is soaring; the investment community has not yet awakened to silver's stark supply/demand facts. This indisputable fact has created an incredible, once-in-a-lifetime opportunity. And you can get there before the alleged insiders, users, and experts.

Those are just a few of the reasons why ignoring gold or silver will cost you a fortune! Gold is headed toward at least $2,200 an ounce (currently near $900, up from $280 so far), and silver is headed for at least $100 (currently more than $14.70, up from $4). I will have more to say about silver in the next chapter. And the best by far is still ahead! You will regret ignoring this epic opportunity for the rest of your life!

Are those forecasts reasonable? Here's food for thought.

In 1981, the historic seventies gold bull market finally topped out at $850. After adjusting for inflation, to merely equal what it did in 1981, gold would have to go (only) to $2,172!

Silver topped out at $50 in 1980. After adjusting for inflation since then, to merely equal what it did in 1981, silver would have to go (only) to $125!

Why then am I so sure that the metals could even go much higher than that? Lots of reasons, but the most compelling is the fact that the biggest single factor that drives gold and silver is monetary inflation, and that's already several times greater now than during the great gold-and-silver bull market of the seventies. And the silver supply phenomenon is a plus that means far higher prices, unless they repealed the law of supply and demand when I wasn't looking.

Why Gold and Silver Now?

1. Real money. Gold and silver (especially silver) have been real money over and over again, in all ages of time and on all continents. Ever since Gutenberg invented the printing press 400 years ago, the world has been littered with worthless dead paper currencies every 50 to 75 years, due to excess money printing. *Every time*, gold and silver became hugely profitable investments, then when the paper currency finally caved in to inflation, they became the only universally acceptable coin of the realm. This was the inevitable result of printing more and more pieces of paper with ink on them, no longer backed by gold or silver, until the public caught on to the scam and would only accept more and more counterfeit money in return for their hard-produced goods and services (price inflation?). And it has happened over and over again throughout history, and "he who refuses to read history is forever condemned to repeat it." Before the inevitable tragic outcomes, monetary inflation has always driven gold and silver.

In the last ten years the Fed has manufactured trillions of dollars out of nothing at by far the fastest pace in history, and it's accelerating. The Fed has then loaned the dollars into circulation, or given them to politicians to spend. This money expansion now dwarfs the monetary explosion which led to that historic metals bull market in the seventies. Gold and silver have been rising recently in response (gold from $252 to $700, and silver from $4 to $12.75).

It's hard for me to exaggerate or overstate what is happening. Economists call this monetary-expansion process "inflation." It really should be called "dilution"—dilution of the money supply, and consequently its value. This inevitably sooner or later causes rising consumer prices, which laymen (and the media—and even Wall Street) will mistakenly call "inflation." Calling rising prices "inflation" is like calling falling trees "hurricanes."

When will the public catch on? That is a gradual, slowly accelerating fact of life, and gold and silver prices are the measurement of public awareness. Sooner or later, awareness becomes a critical mass, and the metals go through the stratosphere.

2. **Falling metals production.** There is a serious supply problem. Twenty years of low or falling gold and silver prices saw a sharp decline in production and exploration of epic proportions, as mining companies had to pull in their horns to preserve their capital. This set the scene for the current great supply problem. Now that prices are high enough to make gold and silver mining profitable again, it will take as much as seven to ten years to develop new mines, and falling supply and rising demand have made higher prices inevitable for the imminent future.

Also, most of the easy silver has been mined over the centuries, even with primitive methods. Most of the shallow, easy-to-mine silver deposits are depleted. For example, during the Roman millennium, they used silver coins for currency and exhausted the Spanish silver mines. Now, as silver industrial applications have soared, there are few substitutes in sight. New silver mines are getting harder and more expensive to find, and supply is falling farther and farther short of demand.

3. Vanishing Inventory. Both metals are far rarer than most people know. All the silver ever mined since the dawn of history, including that in central banks, gold fillings, sunken shipwrecks in the Caribbean, and elsewhere, would cover a football field about four feet deep. It would make a cube about the size of a typical eight-room house. And demand is now leaping past new supplies.

4. Jewelry demand. China and India are enjoying a historic burst of capitalist prosperity, and their booming new middle class is enthusiastically buying gold and silver jewelry, creating soaring new demand.

5. Silver use is incredible and rising. There are now thousands of irreplaceable silver industrial uses, which accounts for the shrinking inventory. Government silver warehouses are now all empty (see the next chapter).

6. Silver is the poor man's gold. Think of gold as large denomination money, and silver as small bills. A one-ounce gold coin is now worth about $750, and you can buy a roll of pre-1965, 90%-silver dimes for close to $50 a roll. Partly because it is so much cheaper, the potential buying pool is much larger, and industrial use is much greater, silver will be more profitable than gold by at least 100%!

Ever since the printing press made paper currency possible, and it eventually failed as it always has, gold and silver as a means of exchange and a store of value have always bounced back. In all ages of time, gold and silver have been symbols of wealth, far more precious in our consciousness than any mere paper. Throughout history, whenever we have lost our confidence in paper decorated with ink—and it inevitably loses its value (inflation)—over and over again we instinctively have turned back to gold and silver.

Born-Again Gold Bug

After more than twenty years of being lukewarm or cool to investing in gold and silver (which turned out to be a good decision), I'm again all-out bullish on the metals, for deeply thought-out reasons. I have written *The Ruff Times* for thirty-two years. It is not written for Wall Street, but for Main Street. When I first began publishing *The Ruff Times* in July 1975, I begged my subscribers to buy $120 gold and $2 silver. Gold finally topped out at $850, and silver went to $35. Then for more than twenty years, I made money for *Ruff Times* subscribers mostly in stocks, bonds, real estate, and other traditional investments.

Partly because of that triumph, and my ongoing counsel during the bull market of the seventies, as to *what kind* of gold to buy, *why* to buy gold and silver, *where* to safely buy them, *The Ruff Times* became by far the biggest financial newsletter in the known universe (over 600,000 subscribers over the years). At the risk of sounding immodest (once I thought I was getting humble; it felt awful, but I was only coming down with the flu), I probably learned at least as much about gold and silver and their markets in that bull run back then as any writer alive today.

But that's only part of the story. Starting early in 1977, the 1977 edition of this book, my mega-bestseller, sold 2.6 million copies, making it the biggest-selling financial book in history. It contained basic reasons why you should buy gold and silver, and helped guide millions of Americans through one of the most profitable investment markets in history. The book was one factor that drove that historic bull market. In the 1980s, after I finally concluded the bull market was over, I then mostly ignored the metals for twenty years (and that was a very good idea as it turned out). Then, in late 1999, I begged people to sell all their stocks, shortly before the spectacular dot.com bubble topped out in April 2000. That bubble is still dot.gone after six years, with Nasdaq down more than 40% since then.

Now I'm back again in familiar territory, riding the "golden calf" since December 2003. As the golden calf becomes a massive bull over the next few years, you can make a ton of money in gold, more than twice as much in silver, and a lot more than that in carefully selected mining stocks. Maybe you missed the boat in the late nineties and didn't get in on the dot.com market. You may feel you missed the chance of a lifetime. There is a new bus coming along every few years, a new bull market made just for you. Well, this is it!

Maybe you got sucked into the stock bubble in the late nineties just before it burst, and then rode out the losses, losing money for months and years until the recent rally topped out in July 2007. Perhaps you feel so traumatized by the experience that you have decided not to take any more investment risks. There is an old saying that "a cat who sits on a hot stove won't sit on one again, but he probably won't sit on a cold one either." The stove is warming, but it's not yet too hot to get on again. So let's discuss a few of the more detailed reasons gold and silver are again safe investments with unlimited potential.

THE TRUE GOLD MYTHS

No other reality-based myth has been as durable as gold. Gold is the classic example of wealth, memorialized in myth and legend. It meant wealth for the Chinese, the Egyptians, the Romans, the Greeks, and the Jews, as did silver. Spanish conquistadors and Portuguese explorers died for them. When the Spanish conquered Central and South America, they sent so much gold back to Europe (when it wasn't being sent to the bottom of the Caribbean in a ship sunk in a storm or by pirates) that the new flood of coins (the money supply) triggered a two-hundred-year inflation in Europe.

We've all heard of the golden boy, the pot of gold at the end of the rainbow, the Midas touch, the silver lining, the golden rule (He who has the gold makes the rules?), the goose that laid the golden egg, and the gold medal for the winner. A flashing gold tooth is a symbol of prestige in many cultures. Golden engagement and wedding rings are recognized all over the world as a symbol of bonding through marriage. In India and the Middle East, gold is often melted down into jewelry and worn for security and as a display of wealth.

UNIQUE CHARACTERISTICS

Gold is more malleable than silver. It can be spun out into a thread that is so thin it is nearly invisible to the naked eye. It can be pounded out into a plate so thin that light can pass through it. It won't rust or corrode. It will look the same in one thousand years as it does now. It bonds well with other metals to form alloys of varying purity, and most of the gold ever mined is still in existence.

Silver is by far the more important industrial metal (see the next chapter). It is used in literally thousands of applications. It can be polished to be more reflective than any other metal, which is why it is used as backing for glass to make mirrors. It has thousands of essential uses in industry. For example, it is an essential component for the manufacture of all audio and video tape, and all film. But above all, it is routinely accepted as money, especially in India, China, and the Middle East.

Controversy

Theodore Butler, an independent silver analyst, says that "silver is in huge short supply, and the shortage is getting worse by the day. The silver inventories which depressed the price for more than sixty years are gone!" Butler is not the only sophisticated silver investor with fixed opinions on the subject. There are other very savvy gold and silver bulls who challenge Butler's supply figures, who believe that silver will rise spectacularly, not because of shrinking supply, but because of rising demand.

Let me make it clear that this controversy is not over whether or not you should invest in silver for great profits, but over the reasons *why*! It's not like Christians arguing with atheists whether or not Christ was the divine Son of God, or even existed. It's more like diverse Christian believers, like Catholics and Southern Baptists, arguing over which has the true Christian theology, but they all believe Christ died for our sins.

EXCHANGE-TRADED FUNDS

One very savvy investor, who has big mining holdings all over the world on at least three continents, believes that the new gold and silver ETFs (exchange-traded funds) mean a big increase in demand. I agree.

The new silver ETF is called ishares **Silver Trust (AMEX: SLV)**, and the gold ETF is called **Streettracks Gold Trust (NYSE: GLD)**. ETFs are a lot like mutual funds, only instead of buying stocks for the ETF portfolio, the fund will have to buy gold or silver bullion as investor money pours in, and unlike mutual funds, you can buy or sell your ETF shares at any hour of the day rather than waiting until the market closes to determine your buy or sell price. They also carry the usual commission for the broker, which will assuage their usual hostility.

This opens up a huge new market for the metals. Until now, brokers have been hostile to the metals for very simple self-interest reasons. Why would they want to recommend that their clients sell some of their stocks, take the money out of the brokerage account, and run off to a coin dealer and put it into bullion where there is nothing in commissions for the broker? Also, until now, main-stream investors have been unwilling to buy bullion because they know too little about it.

Now, the broker can recommend shares of the ETF and make his usual commission, and the money remains in the account. And the investor is now buying silver or gold, but is on familiar-feeling ground. This will unleash a lot of buying power into a very thin market, and is immensely bullish. Demand will soar, and so will the price.

I don't know if Butler is right or not about silver supplies, but I do know the other investors *are* right about demand, and they both may be right! And however the controversy will be resolved by the facts, long-term silver investors may make as much as ten times their money—and maybe a lot more—before it is all done. All sides of the debate agree—we will make a lot of money in silver over the long haul. And remember, silver went from under $2 to $50 in the last bull market, when the consensus was that there was many times more silver than gold above the ground, so the supply figures probably are not the controlling factor. With the ETFs and other factors, demand will surely soar.

One other point my savvy friend made is that silver is "a very dangerous investment," because of its volatility. He's both right and wrong. For the patient long-term investor, silver is not a dangerous investment, because it is very cheap now, and will ultimately go a lot higher. But for the amateur stock day trader and the commodities trader, futures and gold and silver stocks are a no-no for the short-term trader. Why?

DEADLY FUTURES

Let's look at futures contracts first. If you buy a futures contract for any commodity, including gold or silver, you are highly leveraged, and a comparatively small decline can wipe out your "margin," and your broker will then give you perhaps the only free advice he will ever give you—a margin call! You will have to put up more margin money, or you will be liquidated, and there goes your money. That's exactly what happened a year before I first wrote this in 1977. The metals had had a spectacular two weeks, and we were all counting our beautiful profits. Then gold and silver had a hellacious day. For example, silver was down about 14% in one day. There was a raft of margin calls, and a lot of futures traders were wiped out. But holders of the physical metal just worried a little for a few days, if they even knew about it.

How about the mining stocks? I recently got a call from one of my sons who, unbeknownst to me, was day-trading some gold and silver stocks, based on what he thought were my recommendations. He had just gotten whacked in a general retrenchment of the metals. He asked, "Dad, what do I do now?" My answer, "Son, don't ever try to day-trade the gold-mining stocks. They are much too volatile, unless you are quick on your feet and spend the day in front of your computer."

So, are gold and silver dangerous? Only if you are thinking short-term or in leveraged volatile instruments like futures contracts. If you have physical gold or silver or fully owned mining stocks, you just wait it out, or use the dips to buy more. Declines are great opportunities. I will never buy gold or silver futures. The only times I did that over the years, I got my head (and my empty wallet) handed to me. I don't have the temperament or the time to be continually watching the computer screen to be a short-term trader. Amateur futures traders get killed over and over again, until they are broke or just give up.

Even today, I will often meet someone who says, "Howard, I took your advice in the seventies and bought gold and lost a lot of money. I'll never listen to you again." Invariably, upon further questioning, he admits he bought gold futures and got caught in a short-term correction. I never told anyone to buy gold or silver futures for the above reasons. And he wasn't subscribing to *The Ruff Times*, so he didn't know when to sell.

So, what are the lessons here? Avoid futures contracts, unless you are a very quick-on-your-feet trader who is prepared to accept some big losses to balance against the profits to be made later. And never meet a margin call! And, don't try to day-trade the stocks. For futures speculators and day traders, this is a very dangerous market. In the bull market of the seventies, I saw retreats along the way to the eventual huge profits, of as much as 30%. They could wipe out futures traders in minutes.

What is the proper strategy for long-term investors in bullion or stocks? Simple. Be patient and wait out the declines, or treat these temporary declines as opportunities to buy more. I actually lust after those retreats. I will be marketing *The Ruff Times* for a few more years and I want to get my new subscribers into the markets as cheaply as possible.

Gold and Silver Uses

There are serious uses for gold and silver that have little to do with investment, and gold bugs often get the two confused. You need to know the difference.

The metals have three basic uses:

1. Gold and silver coins as personal insurance (noninvestment).

2. Government holdings of gold backing for the currency (noninvestment).

3. Gold and silver for investments when things are right, and only then.

Timing makes no difference with number one and number two. They are for all times and all seasons, not for speculation or investment; but for long-term investments, timing is critical.

GOLD AND SILVER INSURANCE

You should always own gold and silver coins as an insurance policy, during both bull and bear markets. This is a perennial principle—every day, every month, and every year! Like homeowners or automobile insurance, its purpose is to protect you against the possible but unpredictable economic and political calamities that you hope never happen.

It's there to use as real money in the case of a sudden worst-case, like a sudden inflationary currency collapse, or terrorist hackers shutting down the power grid so no one has access to their dollars at the bank or at the ATM, or can't open the supermarket cash registers. It's in case the same terrorist-financed hackers break into the computers of the money-center banks where most of the world's dollars are there in hyperspace, insert a destructive virus, and the world's dollars disappear.

Again remember, only about 5% of the worlds' dollars are minted, printed, or coined. The rest are only on the computers of banks. Three or four years ago, when Kay and I got a home equity (e-lock) loan, they just created the money out of thin air and put the money into our account. We never saw a physical penny of it in the physical world.

If the computer data is wiped out, there could go the monetary system of the world, because the dollar is the world's reserve currency. This would mean the instant collapse of the American economy, and maybe Western civilization. Then the world would instinctively go back to gold and silver as a means of exchange and store of value until the computers are fixed and a new paper-money system is cobbled together.

These things seem to be unthinkable in our otherwise comfortable world. But we have never had such an enemy as Islamo-fascists devoted to America's destruction, with no regard for their personal comfort, well-being, or even their lives. Not even their petrodollars!

INSURANCE ACTION STEPS

Each family should have at least one half-bag of pre-1965, commonly circulated, 90% silver dimes, quarters, and halves (715–725 ounces of silver). "Junk silver" can be bought from any neighborhood coin dealer. In the event of the possible dire world outcomes I have speculated on, gold and silver will explode in value and your insurance coins will become a fantastic investment, which they may not have been when you bought them. In the case of less drastic events, such as mere rising-price inflation, they will also be profitable.

Because of the critical supply/demand situation, as the holder of any form of physical silver, you will find the industries that need them will have to bid up the price until you are willing to part with yours. $100 an ounce, anyone?

This is a buying decision for all seasons, and it only becomes an investment if bad or even mildly bad things (like rising inflation) happen in the world. This is not for short-term profit, but for long-term protection. You would really need it if a monetary crisis or a war gets bad enough and lasts long enough that we have started to universally use coins as the alternative "real" currency. It might not even take that long for merchants to get the drift. During the OPEC gas crisis in the seventies, when inflation and silver were in a runaway mode and gas prices were exploding, a few enterprising gas-station operators were advertising gas for a dime a gallon—pre-

1965, 90% silver dimes—because a silver dime was worth more than the posted gas-price-per-gallon.

Like all insurance, the coins are there to use when bad things happen which you hope won't happen. All insurance is a bet that bad things will happen. You win your bet only if you have a car crash, or a fire, or if you die. With orthodox insurance, it doesn't matter if you win or lose your bet, the premiums are gone forever. In the case of coin insurance, the premiums are still there forever and appreciating, no matter what.

GOLD AND SILVER AS MONETARY BACKING: A CONDENSED HISTORY

In theory, we should be backing our currency with gold and silver, making it fully exchangeable into the metals, like America did for almost two centuries. That's a principled cause that dedicated gold bugs should fight for. While this is very important, it has nothing to do with investing in gold or silver.

Let me repeat. When we began to vote ourselves benefits from the public treasury, government started to print and issue more receipts than there was gold or silver in the warehouses (which we now called "banks"). Who would know, as long as not too many holders of receipts showed up at the bank with their receipts (currency) to demand their gold or silver. And then, we finally thought of the paper receipt (currency) as real money all by itself.

For a long time we had confidence in the "gold and silver backing." But human nature never changes. We soon got so accustomed to our government benefits, paid in receipts, that we accepted the creation of more and more receipts (money). In fact, we were oblivious to the monetary inflation. The only signs were price inflation and rising prices of goods, and rising gold and silver.

Our stage was finally set when it became obvious to foreign dollar-holders that there was not enough metal to meet demands, so they began jostling to be the first in line to present dollars at "the gold window." Panic! Nixon finally faced the reality that there soon would be more receipts (currency) presented for redemption than there was gold available. Until then, foreign governments were still able to exchange their dollars for gold, but we were steadily running out of gold in Fort Knox, as foreign confidence in the paper dollar had sagged so badly due to monetary inflation that we were threatened with soon losing all our gold reserves.

So Nixon closed the "gold window" at the Federal Reserve to stem the tide, and the process was complete; the dollar was now completely detached from gold and silver, and greenbacks were now just a "fiat currency" (money just because a government order, or "fiat," declared that they were real money).

Once we accepted that the horse was out of the barn, there was no longer any worry about whether we had enough gold and silver in the bank to redeem the ever-growing supply of banknotes, and the claims on government "entitlements" were soaring, so inflation was the inevitable consequence of money creation. Along with that, Uncle Sam began an antigold campaign to demonetize the metal and separate it in the public mind from "money." They even began making and marketing gold and silver coins (eagles) as mere commodities. However, enough of us remembered the monetary meaning of gold and silver that they rose at the slightest hint of economic growth and the subsequent threat of inflation. And as gold was an internationally traded commodity, and a lot of foreigners had not bought into the U.S. antigold propaganda, the price began to rise.

"YOU CAN'T GO HOME AGAIN"

Restoring gold backing to the currency would seem to be the obvious solution. In theory, that is so, but that won't work until we are willing to kill the entitlement programs (Medicare, Social Security, Medicaid, etc.), forgo our soaring government benefits and accept the discipline that gold and silver backing provide. We need a sudden rush of brains to the head and character to the heart—and wallet! Don't hold your breath! If you think that will happen, I have a used bridge over the East River to sell you.

It won't happen until the present money system has totally collapsed and we have nothing to lose by replacing it with an honest hard-money system. Now, we collectively feel we have too much to lose. We have a huge vested interest in the status quo—our welfare, our Social Security, our farm subsidies, and other benefits As a matter of principle, we should be in favor of gold backing for money. And this has no relation to whether or not you should invest in gold or silver.

Investing in Gold and Silver

Now let's get to the good stuff—making money with gold and silver.

You should only invest when enough of the essential factors are lined up—like right now. When not enough of the essential elements are there, gold and silver are lousy investments, as they were for two decades. All the factors *are* now lined up, and will remain that way for years. In all probability, you will eventually make money in the metals in the long run, no matter when you bought them or how much you paid for them. Any investment in gold and silver now at almost any price will eventually pay off. Although now the very long-term prospects are just fine, the metals can be near dead for years at a time—like those twenty-two years between the end of the last bull market in 1981 and the beginning of the current one.

In the '80s, when I finally got it through my thick head that the bloom was off the (golden) rose, I waited patiently (impatiently?) for two decades while gold and silver went sideways and down for many years. As it was not the right time for the metals, so we made our money in carefully selected stocks and bonds and real estate for more than two decades while keeping an eye out for today's conditions. So what conditions are now favorable to gold investment?

1. **Money creation** (monetary inflation) must be in a long-term uptrend. That is so right now, and has been the case for years, even during the twenty-two-year metals bear market. So far, so bad, but alone it is not enough to cause a gold bull market.

2. **The dollar losing exchange value against foreign currencies.** This is so essential, that after the dollar was in its current decline, I was finally prompted to turn bullish when I did the final edits on a book in December 2003. Without a weakening dollar on the exchange markets, any moves in the metals will be temporary. Now we have moved beyond that into the next currency phase—the metals rising against *all* currencies, which is super bullish.

3. **War or the prospect of war.** The war against terrorism and the war in Iraq are beginning to meet this condition, al-

though the shooting has been contained locally, mostly in the Middle East. War breaking out further into the world—a terrorist nuclear, biological, or computer-system attack, or Iranian fanatics nuking Tel Aviv—would meet this requirement. We're on the brink, but not there yet. War is a wild card because it triggers inflation due to wartime spending and national and international fear, and is basically unpredictable.

Not *all* of the conditions have to be met at the same time, but conditions 1 and 2 are essential. War just adds fuel to the fire.

Summary

Remember, gold and silver have investment and noninvestment uses, and they are not directly related. It could be argued, however, that gold and silver nonbacking for the currency leads to inflation and all of its ills, and that is true. We could also argue that the insurance-use of junk silver and gold coins can become a profitable investment in a metals' bull market, and that is an added benefit. But buying the metals strictly for investment purposes is not for short-term timing—but for timing long-term bull and bear markets.

Fortunately, now the timing is right, and the golden bull is still a calf, so the decision when to invest in the metals is now a moot question and will be for some years. Just do it!

BAD NEWS BULLS: LOOK FOR THE SILVER LINING

Gold and silver tend to do well when everything else is going to hell. They are a pessimist's dream come true. But for realistic optimists who look for silver (and gold) linings in clouds, bad news is good news indeed. When the stock market or real estate is in the grip of inflation or an inflation-induced recession or depression like we may soon see, or stagflation like we saw in the seventies, gold and silver will thrive. The worse things get, the higher they will go. They are the classic contrarian investment.

When all commodities are in a bull market (like now), gold and silver are the only hard commodities the typical middle-class American can buy. Unlike zinc or copper or steel or soybeans, you don't have to take on a lot of risk like a leveraged futures contract, or have a truck back up to your door and dump a pile of copper on your porch. You can simply go to your corner coin dealer, or call our recommended dealers (see Appendix A), pay cash, and take it home, or simply buy it in the ground—a gold or silver mining stock, like any other stock.

With mining stocks and gold mutual funds, you only have to watch one fundamental—the price of the metals. When they go up, all the mining stocks go up. When the wind blows, even the turkeys fly. Of course, some will fly higher than others for fundamental reasons—production, property potential, management, sufficient capital, and other factors. My job is to help you pick the best (see Appendix A).

Let me digress for a moment for a dissertation on dysfunctional and functional investor attitudes.

POLLYANNA

Too often, journalists who wrote a story about me only read the "Coming Bad Years" of the title of this book. They ignored "How to Prosper."

Pollyanna, the famous literary character, is a case in point. She always saw the bright side of things and ignored the dark side. Partly because of her, we have always thought of those who see the glass as half-full as "good," and those who see the glass as half-empty as "bad." But this has nothing to do with reality. Optimism and pessimism have nothing to do with reality; they are attractive or unattractive emotional states of mind, and may or may not be in tune with the world as it is.

For a further example, gold and silver prosper when things that are considered to be "bad" happen, especially on Wall Street. Associated with gold and silver bull markets are "bad things" such as inflation, war, and stock bear markets. It is natural for brokers to be optimistically bullish on the stock market, no matter what. It is their baby, and the source of their income—commissions. It is also natural for them to reject bullish gold and silver forecasts, which coincide with bearish stock market forecasts. Their clients don't buy stocks when Wall Street is bearish, only when they say that the market is going up. Their views are not rooted in reality, and may be right or wrong at any given time.

For example, just one week before the top of the dot.com bubble in the market in March 2000, a survey of Wall Street advisers and market analysts produced these results: 95% of their recommendations said "buy," and 5% of them said "hold." In less than a month, one of the biggest bear markets in history began. Although the Dow Industrials were in a multiyear rally before this was written, and the Dow not long ago broke to a new high of 14,000 for one day, Nasdaq, which is now much bigger than the Dow, has been down about 40% for seven years from its April 2000 high. During much of this time, Wall Street sentiment has been relentlessly bullish. Sometimes they have been right for a while, sometimes for a year or two at a time, but only because a stopped clock is right twice a day!

That explains why Wall Street is uniformly down on gold and silver. They usually are either actively against it as a holding for their clients, or they act as if it doesn't exist. Until the ETF, they didn't make any commissions on client decisions to own some. They could recommend gold-mining stocks or gold mutual funds, but if they did, there weren't many of them available. Those stocks are a tiny proportion of the stocks available to brokers. If you added up the capitalization of all the gold and silver mining stocks in the world, plus the value of all the metal available to the market and in ETFs, it would be less than the combined market capitalization of Microsoft and Google. A tiny bit of increased volume would bid them out of sight. If all the brokers in the world became gold bugs or silver advocates, there wouldn't be even close to enough merchandise to accommodate them, so their pessimism about the metals is easy to understand, as measured against their self interest. But it has *nothing* to do with reality!

EXCHANGE-TRADED FUNDS (ETFs)

A case in point is an article in the March 31, 2006, *Wall Street Journal*. Silver had just made a dramatic move over the two preceding days and hit the highest price since December 2003. Good news, right? Wrong! The *Journal* missed the point by observing, ". . . it isn't a supply crunch or jewelry demand that is making silver dear." They went on to observe that all this was caused by the imminent approval of the new silver ETF. Now it is true that the silver ETF will probably open up silver investing to more orthodox traders, while providing commissions to brokers, which will cause them to be more likely to recommend it. That's good, and bullish, but not a word in the article about the metals' monetary role and inflation-hedge value. Then the *Journal* proceeded to damn silver with faint praise. They were obviously on uncomfortable ground. I doubt if anyone was converted to silver as a result of that article. But hey, it was better than nothing—almost. I'll take anything we can get.

When I did a recent radio interview, the host, who was basically friendly, said, "You've always liked gold." My response? "No, no, no. I have been bearish for most of two decades before December 2003. In my investment career, I was bullish on gold for my first six years in the newsletter business, then bearish or neutral for two decades. That's bullish for eleven years, and bearish or neutral for twenty years. Now I've been bullish again for more than two years. But I guess I can never shake the label of 'gold bug,' which I earned way back in the seventies."

If you are a realistic optimist like me, you are always looking for the silver (or gold) linings in the gathering clouds, if that is reality. I just want to be right, not because my ego requires it, but because in my profession, being wrong costs me subscribers, or missed opportunities for them. True optimism includes realistically looking for opportunities among bad developments. That is why gold and silver are bad-news bulls!

You can't be bullish about gold and silver if you think everything will be hunky-dory in the world at large. The things that drive the metals are unpleasant for the status quo. I can only be bullish on gold and silver if I believe the dollar will be sinking, inflation will be on the march, the stock market will probably decline, and scary things are happening in the world that will get worse. In that case, a true optimist must look for the aforementioned silver linings.

If the world should suddenly turn sane and the metals should tube, the true optimist will cut his potential losses and look for new opportunities, as I did in the '80s and '90s. When this gold bull market has run its course, if the economy has hung together, we should be able to put the *Wall Street Journal* on the wall, throw darts at it, and invest in the holes the darts pick. But for now, we must invest in silver and gold until it is stock-dart time.

Ironically, gold bugs can be just as ideologically blind as stockbrokers. Many of those who were ideologically turned on to gold because of its insurance uses, or their crusade to reinstall the gold standard, confused those things with gold's merits as an investment. I had loved gold for six years in the '70s, and found it hard to turn seriously bullish about it in the '80s and '90s. Lesson well learned.

Ideology is the enemy of investment, because it obscures reality. You can be a Pollyanna on gold and silver, and may be right or wrong, but not because of your optimism or pessimism. You need to be an optimist to perceive opportunity when things don't measure up to the world you would like to see, as opposed to a realistic view of the world and the markets as they really are. A real optimist knows when to bet the farm when everybody else is expecting a drought, and when not to. Although optimism and pessimism are states of mind, and have nothing to do with truth, they have a lot to do with guts—the ability to be comfortable looking north when everyone else is looking south. I may be wrong about a lot of things, but I try to be driven by realism and objective truth, not some socially approved state of mind.

9

THE SILVER LINING

"The silver lining in every cloud" is the symbol of optimism. It is right up there along with gold and platinum for jewelry or wedding rings. Silver has been by far the most commonly used monetary metal; silver coins are far more common than gold in much smaller denominations. It is the most common coinage used as money; silver coins have been standard currency in many nations in all ages of times, much more even than gold. It has been used more often than gold for coins because many silver deposits are much shallower than gold, so they have been easier and cheaper to mine, even by primitive methods.

But never before have government silver coffers been so bare.

"Silver is used in more applications than any other commodity (aside from petroleum)." Those are the words of Theodore Butler, an independent silver analyst. I agree with Butler that, despite the insanely profitable gold bull market, silver may not be just twice as profitable as gold in the next few years, but even more than that. Why? Butler says, "Silver is in huge short supply, and the shortage is getting worse by the day; the silver inventories which depressed the price for more than sixty years are gone." More about that in a moment. He's certainly right if you are talking about silver *at today's price*.

Unlike gold in the seventies when Jimmy Carter decided that rising gold was an embarrassment to the dollar and announced gold sales from Fort Knox to depress the price, government can't decide to dump their silver onto the market to artificially suppress the price—because they no longer have any! Silver is still the poor man's gold, and the time is not far away when the investment world will finally wake up to the shortages, and the soaring demand will make it difficult to find any investment silver at any price this side of $100 an ounce.

In the inexorable law of supply/demand, price is the great equalizer. There is plenty of silver available—at the right price—and $12 to $15 an ounce is not the right price. At increasingly higher prices, silver jewelry and sterling silver will come out of the woodwork. I remember back in 1980, when I put out my famous silver sell signal, Investment Rarities, which at the time was my only recommended dealer, made millions buying down and melting and salvaging all kinds of silver—sterling silver and bags of coins—as investors who believed me that the silver bull market was over were melting down even heirloom sterling silver.

The same thing will happen again, but at much higher prices. And silver will come out of India and China in the form of jewelry to be melted down, but again, at much higher prices. At these prices, with their economic boom over the last decade, the newly created middle-class Indians and Chinese are buying gold and silver jewelry with their new wealth. Says Butler, "If you could find a commodity which was considered a precious metal and was far more rare than gold, wouldn't today's crazy price discrepancy ($14 for silver and $900 for gold) seem utterly ridiculous?" I agree. But not necessarily for the same reasons as Butler.

When the world discovers the supply-and-demand fundamentals, silver will be the star for investors. The safest money will be made in physical silver held in your possession. Someday soon, the users who need it may not be able to buy physical silver at anywhere near today's price because there won't be any available in the empty warehouses. If they need or want some, they may have to buy yours or metals from India or China—at a much higher price!

Ways to Buy Silver

You have a lot of choices here, some better than others, some good and some just plain bad. Let me count the ways:

1. Junk silver: The government stopped making 90% silver coins after 1964. These commonly circulated (not rare) coins can still be bought from coin dealers by the bag or half bag. A bag contains pre-1965 dimes, quarters, and halves with $1,000 face value, weighs about 55 pounds, and the coins contain 715 to 725 ounces of silver. As this is written, a bag costs a bit more than $10,500 and half a bag is about $5,200. The coin industry calls this "junk silver." They are "circulated," have no numismatic (rarity) value, and you will not pay the face value of the coins, but the current value of the silver in the bag, plus a small premium. Many of them are being scrounged out of circulation and melted down into bullion bars; by the time you read this there may be a rising premium. Pay it. It's worth it!

2. Engelhard silver bullion bars: For larger amounts of silver, you can buy Engelhard 100-ounce bars and store them in a safe depository. They can be bought from any of the coin-and-bullion dealers listed in Appendix A. If they are to be stored anyplace other than where you bought them, or you have taken personal possession of them, they will have to be assayed when you sell them, which can be expensive and time consuming. If they are in storage, be sure they are in trust with an independent trustee as Investment Rarities does (1-800-328-1610). I don't really like them.

3. Silver rounds: Some private mints have manufactured some coinlike "rounds," which you can buy from a coin dealer for very little premium.

4. Semi-numismatic coins: These coins have some of the features of rare coins and bullion. Their price is based on both their rarity, lack of flaws, plus the value of the bullion they contain. They are especially interesting for more than one reason; the numismatic value is based both on their age, and their condition, but the bullion content gives them a price floor, because if they ever lose their scarcity value, they can never be worth less than their bullion value. I really like them a lot. You can buy them from Investment Rarities, or International Collectors Associates (1-800-525-9556).

5. Silver in the ground: Silver mining stocks will be huge winners in the next few years. They are leveraged to the price of bullion, and will grow much faster than coins. They will be like a license to print money! (See chapter 10.)

6. ETFs: Silver ETFs (exchange-traded funds) have been recently launched and are sold on the American Exchange (iShares Silver Trust; AMEX: SLV). It is a convenient way to buy silver. You can buy or sell your shares of the ETF at will, just like stocks. They will trigger a lot of silver buying, and are a very bullish development as it exposes millions of potential, nontraditional investors to silver. ETFs will also have to buy huge amounts of silver to meet their legal obligations, which will be a big demand factor, which is bullish. We'll be watching them closely to be sure they do the required buying.

7. Futures Contracts: Caution! These are heavily leveraged, because you will have to put up only a fraction of the value of the silver in the contract, enabling you to contract for several times as much silver with the same amount of money. As silver goes up, if you don't get a margin call along the way, you will make a lot more money than if you own physical silver. But if it temporarily goes down, you will lose your money a lot faster. If you have 10% margin and silver doubles in price, you will make ten times your money. But if silver goes down 10%, you will lose all your money. Futures are only for those with a lot of money to risk, and nerves of steel. Most of you should avoid them, and the profits in mining stocks may be just as profitably leveraged. The COMEX futures-contract exposure is at least as great as all the known silver bullion inventories in the world.

This form of paper silver will boom pricewise as long as bullion does, but in the long run, by far the most safety will be with physical silver, especially if Butler is right and there isn't enough inventory left for silver users to get delivery settlement on their futures contracts to meet their commercial needs, and they will be forced to raise their bids so they can get you to sell them yours.

WHERE DID THE SILVER GO?

A lot of the world's underground silver deposits were laid down very shallow when God created the earth, so it has been easily mined over the years, even by primitive methods, and most of the world's easy, cheap silver has been dug up. The world is now dependent on increasingly hard-to-find-and-mine deposits. There is continuing production of by-product silver found along with copper, lead, and other minerals. The old, shallow pure silver mines have been depleted or are getting harder and more expensive to mine. Much of the cheap, easy, underground silver is exhausted.

The world's biggest supply of aboveground silver is in India, but it's not in warehouses owned by the government. It is in the form of jewelry. It is a form of wealth worn by millions of Indians. No one person or government can decide to sell some reserves for any reason. It will take mass psychology, and that will take a lot higher prices.

MODERN USAGE

Silver is a ubiquitous and essential industrial metal with literally thousands of uses, many of which are irreplaceable. Jim Cook, president of Investment Rarities (one of our recommended coin dealers, see contact information in Appendix A), has recently listed just a few of silver's thousands of modern uses, many of which are infinitesimal in amounts per unit, but multiplied by many millions of units, it's thousands of tons of silver. (I can't vouch for each one of these statements, but at least most of them are true). This, plus sagging production, largely explains much of Butler's scenario about the disappearing inventories. Let's hear what Jim has to say:

* * *

Both rechargeable and disposable batteries are manufactured with silver alloys. Billions of silver oxide-zinc batteries are supplied to the world's market yearly, including batteries for watches, cameras and small electronic devices, tools, and TV cameras.

Steel bearings are often electroplated with high-purity silver. Silver solder facilitates the joining of materials. Silver-brazing alloys are used in air conditioning, refrigeration, power distribution, automobiles, and airplanes.

Silver is of first importance to plumbers, appliance manufacturers, and electronics.

Chemical reactions use silver as a catalyst; approximately 700 tons of silver are in continuous use in the production of plastics.

Silver is essential for producing a class of plastics which includes adhesives, laminated resins for construction, plywood, particle board finishes, paper and electronic equipment, textiles, surface coating, dinnerware, buttons, casings for appliances, handles and knobs, packaging materials, automotive parts, and electrical insulation materials.

Silver is necessary for producing soft plastics used in polyester textiles. It is used for molded items, for insulating-handles for stoves, and for computers, electrical control knobs, and Mylar tape (which makes up 100% of audio, VCR, and other types of recording tapes). It is also used to produce antifreeze.

Silver is used in commemorative and proof coins around the world. There is wide silver use in silverware, jewelry, and the decorative arts.

Silver is the best electrical conductor of all metals and is used in contacts and fuses and ordinary household wall switches. The use of silver for motor controls is universal in the home, and is even a better conductor of electricity than copper. All of the electrical appliances, timers, thermostats, and some pumps use silver contacts. A typical washing machine requires 16 silver contacts. A fully equipped automobile may have more than 40 silver-tipped switches.

Silver relays are used in washing machines, dryers, automobile accessories, vacuum cleaners, electric drills, elevators, escalators, machine tools, locomotives, marine diesel engines, and oil-drilling motors. It is also used for circuit breakers. It is widely used in electronics, membrane switches, electrically heated automobile windows, and conductive adhesives.

Every time you turn on a microwave oven, a dishwasher, clothes washer, or TV set, you have activated a switch with silver contacts. The majority of computers use silver-membrane switches. They are used for cable television, telephones, microwave ovens, learning toys, and keyboards of typewriters and computers and in prepaid-toll gizmos. These silver-containing, radio-frequency-identification devices will soon make an appearance, embedded in credit cards and passports.

Silver is used in circuit boards and is essential to electronics to control the operation of aircraft, car engines, electrical appliances, security systems, telecommunications networks, mobile telephones, and TV receivers.

Silver is used in windshields in General Motors all-purpose vehicles because it reflects some 70% of solar energy. Every automobile produced in America has a silver ceramic line in the rear window to clear frost and ice.

Silver plating is used in Christmas tree ornaments, cutlery, and hollowware. Because it is virtually 100%-reflective after polishing, it is used in mirrors and coating for glass, cellophane, and metals.

A transparent coating of silver is used on double-paned thermal windows.

Silver has a variety of uses in pharmaceuticals. Silver sulfadiazine is the most powerful compound for burn treatment worldwide. Catheters impregnated with silver diazine eliminate bacteria. It's increasingly being tapped for its bactericidal properties from severe burns to Legionnaire's disease to dressings for wounds.

One out of every seven pairs of prescription sunglasses incorporates silver. Silver-based photography has superior definition and low cost; it is still the biggest user of silver.

Digital photography is considered by many to be a threat to old-fashioned film photography, which at one time was the biggest user of silver, as digital cameras are becoming the camera of choice for millions of people. Ergo, physical silver use will decline in the film business, and that is considered by many to be a bearish factor. Kodak was at one time the world's largest user of silver in manufacturing film. Because they used silver in every roll of film in the seventies, silver photographic use was touted as one reason for the silver bull market of that time.

There is a counterargument, and a counter-counterargument.

It is not generally known, but much of the silver used in film is recycled to be used again by the film companies. That is also true of silver in medical X rays.

But more than offsetting this is the fact that silver is also used in glossy photographic print paper at Wal-Mart, Kmart, and Costco and other supermarkets, for people to print out their digital photos, and that paper is never recycled. One of my daughters informed me that now that she has a digital camera, she takes twelve times as many pictures of the boys as she did with her old-fashioned film camera, and she usually prints them out.

But also, the film companies will still sell 1 billion rolls of film this year.

Silver is widely employed as a bactericide and algaecide. A doctor friend of mine told me that when there is an open wound or big burns, a silver compound is used on the dressing. Silver ions have been used to purify drinking water and swimming pools for generations.

Silver ions in house frames help resist mold and mildew. Silver compounds are providing doctors with powerful clinical treatments against antibiotic-resistant bacteria.

I could go on and on, and I guess I already did, but that's one reason why our silver inventory is under assault, and if Butler is even partly right, that could be one reason why silver is turning into the supply/demand investment of the century.

Will the growing assault on silver inventories trigger a switch to some as-yet-unknown substitutes? In some cases, probably yes. Copper can do some of the things silver can do, but copper is rocketing up in price in a solid bull market, and is becoming a more and more expensive substitute. Usually the thousands of silver uses are so small in each individual unit manufactured that they are only a small part of the cost of manufacturing the units that incorporate it, so there is not enough incentive to change at these prices, but collectively, they add up to thousands of tons of silver.

SILVER AS MONEY

Silver has an important monetary role, according to economic history. One disagreement I have with Butler is that he has discounted the monetary role of silver. Silver has been consistently used as money throughout history, even more than gold, but as I have said several times before, whenever paper money fails (every 50 to 75 years), the world is subsequently littered with useless paper currencies. That's when silver is resurrected and comes back into its own.

For example, when the Chinese government fell at the end of World War II, paper currency became distrusted, but almost like magic, U.S. silver and gold coins became the currency of choice all across that huge, primitive country. Everyone knew what an American silver dime was worth. This held true until the Communists imposed a new "fiat currency" (one that is money just because the government says it is) and enforced it with the heavy hand of government.

Could that happen here in America? No one knows for sure, but that remote possibility is becoming less remote every day. That's why you need some silver for insurance purposes, because the dollar's fate seems to be sealed and delivered by our present rate of internal monetary inflation. Whether it will take one year, 10 years, or 30 years, I don't know, but eventually the world will be littered with worthless paper dollars, and governments will be forced to go back to a gold standard to back a new currency. At some future time silver coins will be minted again in massive quantities, and silver and gold will both reign triumphant over the world's monetary system until we have a monetary system we can trust. I don't know exactly how it will work, and probably nobody else does, either, but for that reason, I repeat, you should buy at least a half-bag of junk silver (pre-1965 American dimes, quarters, and halves) for your family, just for the silver content (about $5200, as this is written). This is not for investment (even though it will go up), but as an insurance policy against a possible inflationary calamity.

Silver always rises during gold bull markets, usually twice as far and fast as gold, but the supply/demand situation (ETFs and jewelry and industrial usage) dwarfs all other reasons why silver will soar in price, perhaps much more than twice as much as gold.

The government coffers are now empty. In the seventies, Jimmy Carter announced they would be dumping some of the gold at Fort Knox into the market to depress the price, because rising gold was considered an embarrassment to the government. This time Uncle Sam can't dump silver on the market to try to manipulate the price, or use his own inventory to make silver coins, because he doesn't have any. And he doesn't have a good reason to do so.

One other supply/demand factor that really matters is that COMEX (the New York Commodity Exchange), by far the biggest commodity exchange in the world, has a monster silver futures exposure. Many of the "longs" have bought a silver contract from the shorts contracting for the silver, in the hopes that silver will be rising, and so will their contract. It can be settled either with a cash payment or by delivery of the physical metal. But a lot of the longs are silver users who need the metal and have only bought the contracts for delivery.

They won't settle for cash, but only for delivery, because they need the metal.

The "shorts" have sold silver they don't have, assuming they will be able to buy it back at a lower cost in the future and thereby profit handsomely. They are pure speculators, betting that the price will go down so they can buy it cheap. Steadily rising prices are their worst nightmare.

The longs are even more dangerous than the shorts. Remember, for every long contract, there is a corresponding short. As silver has soared, shorting paper losses have mounted to many billions of dollars.

I guess the short speculators never learn. That's exactly what they did back in the seventies, and when the Hunt brothers tried to corner the silver market and drove the price to $50, most of the governors of the COMEX were short, in effect betting against the Hunts. Their losses mounted day by day, and as they became more and more insolvent, their need to cover their shorts, either with cash or by buying silver to deliver, was way beyond their financial ability to handle. Technically the COMEX should have been shut down, as many of the shorts were governors of the COMEX, but this was unthinkable, as we couldn't allow the world's most important commodity exchange to close down.

Eventually they won the battle with the Hunts by, among other things, changing the rules to "liquidation only." That's when I decided to tell my subscribers to sell their gold and silver at $35 an ounce, before the $50 top, as when the elephants are fighting, we mice should scurry into the underbrush. Yes it went to $50, but $2 to $35 is good enough.

This is similar to where COMEX finds itself today. But this time they are short so much silver, that if they had to buy enough silver to cover all their shorts, especially if the longs are silver users who need the physical silver for their industries (many are) and won't accept just a cash settlement, that this could soak up as much as 100% of all silver production. Also, the short's cash position is so dire, as their paper losses have mounted as silver has risen, that they won't have enough money for a cash settlement. Sooner or later they will have to buy silver, and the stability price of silver could soon be above $100 an ounce (my best guess) in order to induce holders (you) to give up yours.

Silver is the investment of the century. It will move with gold, but farther, as has already been demonstrated. Gold is up about 300%, and silver is up more than 500% over the last couple of years. We will eventually find that silver at today's $12 to $16 is the bargain of the century. Silver and silver-mining stocks will be a license to print money.

For silver bullion coins or semi-numismatic coins, contact Investment Rarities by calling (800-328-1860); International Collector's Association (800-525-9556); Kitco (877-775-4826); or Camino Coins (800-982-7070). Always compare prices. They are all dependable and long-standing friends of mine. Prices may differ one way or the other on any given day. You don't necessarily need the very cheapest; close is good enough. I beg you on bended knee to buy silver! This is the safest investment call I have ever made.

10

MINING STOCKS: A LICENSE TO PRINT MONEY

Now let's get just a bit more sophisticated in our pursuit of profits. History has shown us that in a metals bull market you will make a lot more money in silver than you will in gold, but you will make more than twice as much money in selected gold- and silver-mining stocks as you will in silver. Why? Because they are uniquely leveraged in relation to pure bullion. More about that in a moment.

I have prepared this chapter with the indispensable help of James Raby of National Securities (1-800-431-4488). He is a consummate pro, and he has forgotten more about mining stocks than you and I will never know. On second thought, I take that back; I don't think he has forgotten anything! The typical stockbroker knows little or nothing about mining stocks, and is often forbidden by his company to trade Canadian stocks, where some of the best values are found. Raby trades both.

Some of the best capital-gains possibilities are young companies listed only in Canada. The symbols include T, TO (the Toronto Exchange) or V or TV (Toronto Ventures, the old Vancouver Exchange, now a subsidiary of Toronto). If your broker can't do business in Canada, you will miss out on some of the greatest speculative opportunities, where the long-term return might be 1500% or more, as opposed to 500%.

Often the first listing of a publicly traded mining company is in Canada. As more is known through the development process, they will graduate from Canada to the Bulletin Board in the U.S., then perhaps to Nasdaq, then to the American Exchange with the cost of admission getting progressively higher.

The Genesis of a New Mining Company

All mining companies have to start somewhere, and it might be helpful for the new investor to understand their origins.

To make money in the mining business, you have to invest in good people; the better the people, the better the odds of locating and acquiring good property. The properties are usually hundreds if not thousands of acres.

Once the prospective property is found, the mining companies start digging surface trenches and establishing drill targets with assays of trench samples. This can be very costly and requires geologists, lab tests, and so on.

Financing all of this can be time-consuming and complex, and it has to be paid for by someone. Once the company has a good idea of the ore body—assuming good results—additional drilling will be done to get as detailed a picture as possible.

Soon a preliminary "inferred resource" calculation is made. This is essentially a crude estimate of what is in the ground.

Next comes a feasibility study. Then quite often a major mining company will take an interest and conduct their own feasibility studies to decide if they want to invest in or buy the project to replenish their reserves. As good news comes in, the price of the stock moves up, but conversely, the leverage for investors decreases. The more you are willing to risk early in the game when less is known, the lower the price, and the bigger your possible gains. Conversely, the more extensive the improvements, the more likely the price will be higher, thus a lower opportunity for large gains. Companies in the development stage offer a unique opportunity to literally get in near the ground floor.

Investors in exploration and development stocks will take more risks with their money, but the upside can be astronomical. Possible huge returns are what draw people into the junior-mining sector, even though these properties can take years to become producing mines.

LEVERAGE

Now let's look at the leverage that is routinely found in a gold or silver mine. Let's do the math. Follow me carefully, because this is the key to understanding why you will make a lot more money in stocks in a gold or silver bull market than you would in just bullion.

Let's assume you own some gold bullion at $350 an ounce, and gold goes to $400. Your $50 profit (at least on paper) is about 14%.

But now, let's assume you are a shareholder of a mining company that produces gold at $300 an ounce and gold is now at

$350; the mine is currently making $50 an ounce on every ounce it produces, but if gold goes to $400, they are now making $100 an ounce. The profits have doubled! That's a 100% increase in profitability, so your stock probably will at least double!

That's 100%-plus, compared to 14%! That's about seven times better! Historically, a development or exploration company that strikes it rich may eventually give you 15 or 20 times as much profit as bullion. That's why I said that mining stocks may be like a license to print money!

THE MINING STOCK PYRAMID

There is a strategy I call, "playing the pyramid." Early in the bull market, the first stocks to rise will be the blue chips with low production costs at the top of the pyramid. Many of those companies are so big that when they open a new mine, this will have less impact on profits than a smaller company might enjoy from a new mine.

As gold rises, you can move down the pyramid to shares of the high-cost production companies that have just become profitable as the price of gold rises above their profit threshold. This gives you more leverage, as a 5% move in gold could mean as much as a 100% increase in mining profits and a big run-up in their stock.

You can in effect start at the top with the biggest, most stable producers and work down. You should probably start with Newmont (NEM-NYSE).

As you move down the pyramid, both the risk and the potential profit increase.

Another strategy is to diversify across the whole spectrum from top to bottom. Then as the market matures over time, shift the weight of your allocation toward the bottom of the pyramid—the development and exploration companies. An Investment Menu is listed in Appendix A.

Also, a gold or silver strike, or the acquisition of a development company with proven reserves, can have a greater impact on the production and profits of small to medium producers than it would on a giant blue chip mining company. It will be a windfall for both the acquiring company and the shareholders of the acquired company. Holding the shares of an acquisition prospect can be a huge windfall. I'll keep up on the potential merger deals, and report on them in *The Ruff Times* (www.rufftimes2.com).

Silver mining stocks should be the stars. Big changes will occur as the market matures. There will be many acquisitions, mergers and barren holes, as well as upside surprises. I will track all of this in *The Ruff Times* and will also have articles from some other writers who have further enlightenment and choices in addition to what I have offered here.

The Investment Menu in Appendix A covers the major categories, although some of them cross the lines, so I'll do the best I can. This list is not a portfolio, but an a la carte menu for you to choose from. This is not a complete list, but a selected, limited list, and it is a moving target. It reflects the market as it is now. A year from now this list may be partially obsolete. I will stay abreast of the changes and continually publish an expanded and a continually revised list in *The Ruff Times*.

To avoid going down deep and coming up dry, I have included only a partial list in the appendix. There are more in my newsletter, especially in the development and exploration categories. I have included here only those which are most likely to still be on the menu a year from now.

POLITICAL RISK

This is not the conventional gold-bug wisdom, but I am a bit concerned with political risk in the undeveloped world. As exploration has gone further and further afield, more and more of these companies are in places like primitive Africa, China, Vietnam, and South America. These companies are only as sound as their relations with sometimes-volatile governments.

Recently, for instance, Chavez, the Marxist madman who runs Venezuela, has seized control of the American Oil companies operating in Venezuela. The newly elected Marxist president of Bolivia has recently nationalized all the foreign gas companies doing business in Bolivia.

Is this the wave of the future for mining companies? I don't know, but as they become more and more profitable, they will be very tempting targets for expropriation. When Bolivia made their announcement, the stock of Apex Silver, which has big Bolivian holdings, took a beating because of concern over their future.

For that reason, I would assign a smaller portion of my portfolio to companies with big operations in potentially unstable countries, and concentrate most of my money on companies with American and Canadian mines, and there are plenty of them. Don't ignore the foreign companies completely, just be a bit cautious.

OTHER CAUTIONS

Not all management teams have the same degree of qualification, experience, and integrity. My job is to help sort out the sheep from the goats so you can make good picks, but it is foolish to try to decide which mine will be the best performer. I'm not smart enough to do that. I suggest you start your own small mutual fund by making a list of my recommended mining companies, posting the list on the wall, throwing ten darts at it, and then dividing the money up among the holes in the dart board. As you gather more experience over time, you will see which stocks are performing the best, and then you can prune your list and concentrate your money in three or four of the best ones. The odds are that they will all rise, but not equally. The key is to spread your risk, then concentrate on the winners.

Not too long ago I spoke at a gold-investment conference in San Francisco, and the exhibit hall was loaded with small mining companies looking for investors. They all had great stories. If you go to one of these conferences, make a list of the exhibiting companies and use my dartboard method. Never try to pick just one given mine.

Remember: "When the wind blows, even the turkeys fly" and "A rising tides raises all boats," and I will do my best to sort out the biggest winners. The cream will rise to the top, although early in the game, the scum also rises. The cream will remain, and the scum will dissipate.

I will write regularly in *The Ruff Times* about these mines, and there is much to learn. But they are as easy to buy as any stock because they are generally listed over-the-counter or on an exchange. Some of the less-mature stocks are listed on the Toronto Ventures exchange (the old Vancouver Exchange). Many blue chip mining stocks are also listed every day in the *Wall Street Journal* on the American or New York Stock Exchanges.

You can buy the stocks through any broker, but again, I suggest James Raby at National Securities (800-431-4488).

This category can be loaded with opportunity, with picks ranging from conservative to highly speculative. Sometimes the first stocks to move are not necessarily the best ones, just the ones with the best PR and marketing. We will try to steer clear of those. Some of the best will be laggards for a while because they are more concerned with running a mining company and doing sound exploration and drilling than they are with cultivating investors. Sometimes they are well financed, have worked out partnership deals with major companies, and sooner or later the world will discover them and they will outperform many of the early winners.

This is an immensely profitable game. But don't forget that your safest course of action will be to buy gold and silver coins and take them home. You should buy gold and silver in the ground only after you have taken care of your insurance and basic investment positions with coins and bullion. But of course, that is all up to you. If you are a novice at the mining-stock game, start conservatively with the giants, like Newmont or Hecla.

But remember, as your growing knowledge adds to your confidence, mining stocks in this gold and silver bear market may be your once-in-a-lifetime chance to get sincerely rich investing.

11

THE OLD HOMESTEAD

In the first edition of this book, in 1977, I recommended real estate as an inflation hedge, and especially recommended small-town real estate. Given recent developments, that recommendation has to be modified.

Residential real estate will eventually be a great inflation hedge, but only after the current bust in real estate has run its course, which it is doing as I write. Small-town real estate will eventually be the place to go. By small town, I don't mean just little towns of 2,000 or 3,000 people, but medium-size communities, as opposed to megalopolises like New York City, Los Angeles, Chicago, San Francisco, Boston, and so on. By "small-town real estate," I mean farther out on the edges of those cities, where housing will become affordable. A lot of this depends on whether or not we are able to develop cost-efficient fuel substitutes for oil and much more efficient cars—to offset the inevitable rise in oil prices that will drive up gas at the gas pump—keeping suburbs viable places to live.

Starting in 2004, I started warning my subscribers about

a coming real estate collapse. The conventional wisdom of many of those who agreed with me was that it would be limited to those areas of the country where prices had soared to unreasonable levels, like California, Nevada, Arizona, Florida, and the Northeast (New England, New York, Philadelphia, around Washington D.C.), the Chicago area, and a few other places.

According to them, it would be a natural correction from inflated prices, caused by various factors (speculation in Florida, for example). We now know that it wasn't so much a real estate price bubble as a debt bubble caused primarily by the Fed driving rates to 1% for years, to offset the dot.com stock market crash of 2000 and prevent a depression. Mortgage rates under 4% encouraged people to buy bigger homes than they really needed. They would gauge their purchase by whether they could afford the monthly payments on big houses, which had been driven down and down by low interest rates and aggressive mortgage lenders.

The bait was the plethora of creative mortgages with even lower initial rates—ARMs (adjustable-rate mortgages) and interest-only ARMs—and the concealed hook was the fact that if rates went up, payments would go up, reducing the number of people who would qualify for a loan, or the size of the house they could buy, creating a swelling number of foreclosures by those who could not meet their rising mortgage payments, and shrinking the buyers' market.

Also, millions were sucked into refinancing their homes, taking advantage of soaring home values, using tax-deductible ARMs and interest-only loans, so they could spend the new cash on upgrading their homes and buying better cars and more consumer gadgets. Much credit for the booming economy was given to the Bush tax-rate cuts, and they deserve some of the credit, but the real driving force was the boom in real estate and the subsequent refinance-driven consumer spending, driven by the low interest rates.

Then the Fed began to worry about the rising inflation that they themselves had caused by the orgy of buying and refinancing they had themselves triggered, and they decided to raise rates, supposedly to fight the incipient inflation. Suddenly millions of homeowners with ARMs and interest-only loans found their payments going up, and foreclosure rates started to rise as millions of others found that their budgets were being squeezed.

Here are some scary numbers as of 2005:

- 32.6% of new mortgages and home equity loans in 2005 were interest-only, up from 0.6% in 2000.

- 43% of first-time home buyers in 2005 put no money down.

- 15.2% of 2005 buyers owe at least 10% more than their home is worth (negative equity).

- 10% of all homeowners with mortgages have no equity in their homes (zero equity).

- $2.7 trillion in loans will adjust to higher rates in 2007 and 2008.

These facts sank in and started to slash consumer spending, and tubed real estate buying and refinancing. New home and used home buying hit a stone wall, with sales down an average of 9% in twenty-nine states, with worse to come.

When a real estate bubble implodes, the first thing that happens is that the inventory of homes for sale starts to rise, and it takes longer and longer to sell a home. Then as supply exceeds demand, sellers start to panic and reduce prices. Then a trickle becomes an avalanche. Home prices are collapsing and equity is disappearing down the memory hole, even in less inflated areas. The reasons are manifold, but the one that is most likely to affect you is that when interest rates rose, a lot of people who had refinanced their homes with ARMs and spent the money on entertainment centers and new cars, found themselves unable to make the monthly payments on their ARMs.

Remember that a mortgage is not owed by the house, but by the owner—the house is merely collateral. One of the big mistakes "prudent" people have made is to add to their monthly payments, adding to their equity. But equity is a nonproducing asset. It not only doesn't produce any revenue for you, but it costs you money every month. So rising interest rates have had the negative impact that I thought they would, after the recent orgy of real estate borrowing to fund consumer spending. In the previous hottest areas, speculative buying has collapsed, as speculators even walk away from their speculative down payments when they find they can't resell their homes.

There are serious foreclosure problems virtually everywhere you look. The *Wall Street Journal* reported on August 19, 2007, that there are huge increases in mortgage defaults in places like Stockton, Atlanta, Fort Lauderdale, Tampa, Las Vegas, San Bernardino, Fort Smith (Arkansas), San Luis Obispo, and Fayette (Arkansas). The delinquency rate is now 2.33% (2007), which is up .30% since December 31, 2005. Now that doesn't sound very bad, unless you have been forced into foreclosure and lost all your equity.

There is no satisfaction from having been right about this.

Real estate is collapsing, equity is disappearing into cyberspace as prices go down, and it has a few years to go until residential real estate will bottom out and make sense as an inflation hedge. I will keep track in *The Ruff Times*. Even if you live in an area that hasn't overly inflated, you cannot escape the effect of increases in interest rates if you have an ARM, or shrinking equity because of the foreclosures around you, triggered by those who have ARMs and have watched their equity disappear, often through foreclosures.

So What to Do?

I have done some recent articles in *The Ruff Times* that will cut the ground out from under your old-fashioned real-estate strategies and even some of the things I have advised over the years. The world has changed, and certain new strategies can take advantage of the new world in which we live.

ARBITRAGE

Banks make fortunes by borrowing at one rate from depositors and loaning it at higher rates to borrowers. It's a safe way for them to make money, and it shows how debt, properly managed, can be a source of great wealth. You can also do it.

Paying down your mortgage can be a poor strategy. Your monthly payments will not go down and the bank won't be forgiving when you get in trouble, despite your extra payments, because of the bad economy or your pension plan defaulting, or your income is cut just because you have gotten older and retired. One woman said it all: "Since my husband retired, I have half as much income and twice as much husband." That's happening to a lot of people, and a lot of my readers are older.

The new strategy can be summed up in a few words: You should have the largest possible mortgage, and the cash should not be spent on things of diminishing value such as home entertainment centers, big flat-screen TVs, or vacations. It should be put to work earning more than it costs you, just like the banks do when they borrow from depositors. You can become an arbitrager.

Home equity is a nonproducing asset. It costs you money, and even as you pay your mortgage down, your payments don't go down, they remain the same as they were when you made your very first payment, even though you have made conscientious efforts to increase your equity, say paying extra on the principal every month. If you fall on hard times and go to the bank and say, "We have even been making extra payments, so can't you give us a break for a few months?" Fat chance!

FACING REALITY

The reality is that the bloom is off the real estate rose for a few years. New buyers are in many cases shut out of the market just by their inability to make the increased payments that follow rising interest rates as night follows the day. They have to buy smaller houses, or no house and rent, so the market will crumble from the bottom up.

Borrow against as much of your costly, nonproducing equity as you possibly can and put it to work in safe, income-producing investments or inflation hedges. Your mortgage-loan interest payments are tax-deductible, which reduces the net cost of borrowing by as much as 30%. It is also simple interest. You can put the money to work, even at a lower stated rate, as long as it is in a safe, secure place, like a money-market fund, because that will be compound interest, or even in gold, silver, or mining stocks for capital gains. You can actually increase your net worth, converting your equity from a fallow, nonproducing, cost-producing asset into an income-producing or capital-gains-producing asset.

In the meantime, we are nowhere near a bargain basement to make a home a reasonably priced inflation hedge. Inflation hedges are supposed to go up, not down. The real estate market will keep falling apart for one simple reason: When you have a bursting real estate bubble, the first thing that happens is that speculators tend to fade away as interest rates go up, increasing their costs. The listing books get thicker and thicker, and it takes longer and longer to sell a home. The last thing to happen is that actual prices fall as most people endure a breaking-down market for a while, assuming that it is merely transitory and a short-term problem. If they could just "wait awhile" a buyer will sooner or later show up.

People are finally forced to face reality that the real-estate market will not go back up for a few years. The only way they will sell their home is to cut the price. We sold our home below the market. Six months later I was thrilled with that decision, as the bigger price cuts materialized and reality set in.

The best way to deal with a declining market is to make sure your equity is safely out and making money for you rather than disappearing as the value of the property drops. So borrowing against the property and putting it to work is a sound strategy. Spending the money on "things" is a bad strategy. I have now borrowed against my northern Utah home and invested the money. The market is still in good shape here, so we were able to get a pretty good but inexpensive loan.

The *Wall Street Journal* recently did a long article on one of the fastest-growing segments of our economy—the rich are increasing their debt faster than the middle class, mostly against their mansions. There is one big difference, however. The middle class is spending its mortgage proceeds on consumption! The rich look upon their debt as a financial tool, so they rarely own their homes outright, even if they can. Instead, they are mortgaged to the hilt with the money at work. The banks do it all the time; they borrow from depositors at one low rate and loan money to borrowers at a higher rate.

So the rich are piling on debt faster than the middle class, though for very different reasons. The middle class are borrowing to maintain their lifestyle; they are basically consuming their assets so they can have more house, better and newer cars, home theaters, and other things. Borrowing by the rich is a tool to increase their wealth, as a contrast.

According to the Federal Reserve, the nation's richest 1% loaded up on $342 billion in new debt between 1998 and 2004. Just as the rich control a disproportionate share of national wealth, they also account for a disproportionate share of debt. The richest 1% now holds 7% of the nation's debt, for a total of $650 billion in borrowing. Debt for this group grew faster than for any other group in the debt survey. The rich are borrowing to increase their capital. They are what the *Wall Street Journal* calls "the leveraged elite." Their debt is used as a way to expand their fortunes.

Unlike many lower-income Americans who rely on credit cards, home equity, and other loans to pay living costs, the rich often use debt as a financial tool. Most of their debt is for mortgages on their primary or nonprimary residences. They have the cash to pay for their million-dollar mansions, but they would rather keep their mortgage money in high-return investments or their businesses. So, the borrowing by the rich is not only a way of increasing their income, but in a real estate decline it has the added benefit of making their equity "fixed" instead of eroding in a declining market. On the whole, the balance sheets of the wealthy remain healthy.

In a world awash in cash, many of today's wealthy made their fortunes by leveraging and making big bets with their business. They have applied the same principles to their personal loans. I would suggest that you imitate the rich in this respect; I am suggesting that if you borrow to the hilt against your equity, and you are conservative, you can put your money in a money-market fund where the principal remains fixed and the compounded yield exceeds the tax-deductible mortgage costs, or in your business.

One wealthy borrower calculates whether a loan makes economic sense. "I won't just go out and borrow money to buy a boat because there is no economic justification for that, but if I can make more than my borrowing costs for a loan, I will consider it. My litmus test is that if I can't pay it back in a worst-case scenario, I won't borrow it."

The advantage of this strategy for the American middle class is that if they are conservative, they are keeping their equity intact so if they ever wanted to pay it off and put their equity back into the house when this real estate decline ends, they could immediately do it with the capital they safely parked in, for example, a money-market fund. This flies in the face not only of conventional financial wisdom, but in the face of some things I have recommended in the past. For example, in most cases you shouldn't have an interest-only loan, but in this case maybe you should, because if you are merely paying interest, your monthly cash outlay will be lower, the tax benefits will stay the same, and the earnings in your money-market fund will remain constant.

Just make sure you are earning more than your mortgage payments.

One disadvantage of this strategy is that it could produce negative cash flow, because you will have to make your monthly mortgage payments no matter what. If you want the maximum return from your money-market fund yield, you have to compound it, which means letting the interest accumulate in the fund so you can earn compound interest (interest on interest).

So the interest you are paying for the mortgage may be negative cash flow, but your net worth is increasing, so consider the payments on your mortgage to be a form of contribution to your retirement fund. In the meantime, seriously consider this strategy in any down real estate market for the following reason: 1) it freezes your equity at a fixed amount so it is no longer subject to declines triggered by a sagging real estate market; 2) it is "arbitrage," which can actually increase your net worth month after month, year after year, and that's exactly what the rich do.

The Beat Goes On

The homeowner vacancy rate (HVR) has climbed to its highest level since the Census Bureau began tracking it four decades ago. Recently the Census Bureau said that in the final three months of 2006 there were about 2.1 million vacant homes for sale. This brought the national homeowner vacancy rate to 2.7%, up from 2.0% a year earlier. Before 2006 the number had never risen above 2.0%. It's still rising.

This varies by region. The South had an HVR of 3.0%, the Midwest had a rate of 2.9%, the West had a 2.4% rate, and the Northeast had a rate of 2.0%. This report, which usually gets little attention, reinforced my growing concerns about the housing market. One economist said the rising vacancy rate of excess housing supplies continues to grow. This vacant housing stock attacks the value of everyone's home equity as sellers slash prices to move their vacant properties, driving down everyone's home equities, including yours.

THE BOTTOM LINE

The bottom line is this: housing values are dropping and will continue to drop, and you should seriously consider my strategy for freezing your equity until the slide has bottomed out. When the market drops, the lenders aren't hurt as long as you are making your payments, but the homeowner is hurt because each drop immediately carves up his equity.

I am not referring to money-market accounts at banks, which are *not* money-market funds. *Real* money-market funds are required by law to keep their principal constant, so you would show absolutely no losses regardless of what the real estate market does. In fact, rising interest rates are excellent for money-market funds because they increase the yields every month. Money-market funds can turn over their portfolio in as little as every month, which means that in a rising interest-rate market, the yields are going up, up, up, while the principal is remaining constant.

SAVING YOUR EQUITY

For most of you, the biggest financial events of 2007, 2008, and beyond (along with inflation and the metals) will be the steady erosion of what you consider your biggest, safest asset—your home equity. Let's consider how much you would be willing to deposit into an investment account with the following features:

- The customer can pay more than the minimum monthly contribution, but not less.

- If a customer attempts to pay less, the financial institution keeps all of the previous contributions.

- The money in the account is not liquid; you can't get your hands on it when you want to.

- The money deposited into the account is not safe from the loss of principal to market conditions.

- Each contribution made to the account results in less safety of principal.

- The money deposited into the account earns a zero rate of return.

- The customer's income-tax benefit decreases with each new contribution.

- When the plan is fully funded, there is no income paid out to the customer. It has a zero yield, so you could only realize your profits by the sale of your investment.

That's why home equity is an extremely unappealing investment. Would you invest serious cash into such an investment account?

There are two places most people accumulate the most money or value: 1) their retirement account; and 2) their home. Since the home is the single largest investment most Americans make during their lifetime, let's explore why home equity is not now a prudent investment.

How can you learn to manage your equity better to increase liquidity, safety, and a rate of return. The above is taken from two most interesting books, which I recommend you get: *Missed Fortune* and *Missed Fortune 101* by Douglas R. Andrews. They are available wherever fine books are sold. This relatively revolutionary strategy is not new. Millionaires and billionaires have done this forever. None of the really big moneymakers of the world would have huge equities in their homes. They maintain the largest amount of indebtedness, deduct the tax-deductible interest payments, and invest the borrowed money elsewhere. Even on your smaller scale, the principle works.

There are four financial matters that will make headlines in the next few years: 1) shrinking home equity; 2) inflation; 3) gold and silver; and 4) rising interest rates. I've struggled with accepting this radical concept, but the numbers are inexorable and irrefutable. This can increase your return on your home way beyond the dubious capital increase in value over the next few years. In fact, there will probably be no capital increase under current market conditions, only losses. If your equity money is not detached from your home by borrowing against the home and putting it to work with a positive arbitrage return, your home is becoming a crummy investment. If you follow my strategy, it will remain a wonderful investment.

These views will be borne out over the next few years.

WHY YOUR HOME?

There are many fine real estate newsletters and books discussing how to make money investing in real estate, but that's not what I'm interested in at the moment. I want you to keep the value of probably your largest investment, so you can dive into inflation-hedge investments now, and real estate as an inflation hedge when the time comes. At times like this when the value of real estate is being eroded by the market, you need strategies that will help keep you from losing a large portion of your personal wealth.

There are too many ways to make money that don't cost you anything, or at the very most, nominal amounts over the years. So your home has to be measured by other standards:

1. It's your castle. It's the place where you live and need to feel secure. Ideally, the best emotional position would be to own it free and clear so no banker or lender can foreclose on you if your income is interrupted and take it away from you. It can be ultimate security if it's free and clear.

2. It's the place where you live or grew up; it has emotional implications. How many of us have been touched when we visited the house where we spent our childhood? Our home is our secure castle.

3. We think of it as an investment simply because it appreciates, but do the math. Subtract the monthly costs in debt service, maintenance, and other expenses from the appreciation and you will see the returns are a lot more modest than you think, unless you go through some exceptional years like 1995–2003. And there is no yield unless you sell.

When real estate goes through periodic declines, as it is doing now, your shrinking equity chews away at your net worth.

George Soros is an enemy of the political right, and for that

I despise and fear him; however, he is one of the most brilliant investors of all times. He is a billionaire by investing. He almost brought down the Bank of England by speculating on the pound sterling. One of his close associates recently reiterated exactly how I feel when he said that "We have no idea how bad the real estate decline will get." Yes, the decline will be hideous, and will strike at the roots of what you thought was your secure core of wealth.

When the market falls, the people who basically own the bulk of your house, the lenders, are unaffected. Your loan is not paid by your house, it is being paid by you and must be paid no matter what, unless you want to lose your home.

Perhaps the best position of all is to own your home free and clear with no debt.

The second position (probably yours) is the most dangerous, and that is to have a small amount of debt with a large amount of equity and little liquid cash. If you have been sharply paying down your mortgage, you are in no-man's-land in a very dangerous position. If you were a real estate lender and the market got into trouble and you were faced with a lot of foreclosures, would you be interested in foreclosing on a property with small debt and large equity or large debt and small equity? The smaller your debt, the more vulnerable your position. The lender will want to take over a $100,000 house if he has to write off only a $20,000 mortgage to acquire an $80,000 equity, as opposed to writing off an $80,000 loan to acquire a $20,000 equity. It's a simple matter of math.

If you're in that no-man's-land between owning a home completely free and clear, and having a small mortgage and a large equity, that's dangerous. The people who control your life, the mortgage lenders, look with lustful eyes upon your equity.

It is amazing how much resistance I've had with my conservative subscribers over this strategy. But the past real estate clichés have been pounded into them, and they don't realize that the world has changed, and we must change with it. Home values sometimes go down. Many subscribers think I'm a heretic because I am suggesting you borrow out your equity and put the money to work, giving you a return, which real estate equity does not now do. You now have no return on your equity.

We don't have just a subprime lending problem; it affects everyone clear up and down the line who has home equity. It will be a lot worse than you think. 12.4% of all subprime borrowers were at least 60 days late on their mortgage payments in February 2007, the highest level since they began tracking it in 1989. Additionally, 14.3% of subprime loans sold by Wall Street were at least 60 days behind in payments in January, the highest level for securitized "subprime" mortgages since they began tracking them in 1997. I believe that lower home prices could be as much as 40% below today. Don't feel too good if your neighborhood seems to have escaped the carnage. Just wait.

SO WHAT COULD GO WRONG WITH A MONEY-MARKET FUND?

Interest rates could go down, reducing your yield to less than your mortgage payment, in which case you can liquidate your investment and pay off your mortgage.

WHY DO I FEEL THIS WAY?

So why do I expect lower real estate prices and rising interest rates?

In the Phoenix area where my daughter Sharon lives, homes once sold so fast that sometimes when the listing hit the multiple-listing service (MLS), that very same morning several buyers would show up, who were often willing to pay more than the asking price. Well, the bloom is off that rose. Phoenix home sellers now wait for months to sell at lower prices. It was strictly a bursting Fed-induced bubble, partly because interest rates rose, pricing many out of being able to afford a home, and ARM rates started resetting, causing a rash of foreclosures.

The bursting of the real-estate bubble is a big-time deal, and it won't fix itself in a matter of a few months. It will take years before the market bottoms out. Real estate will some-day again be a great inflation hedge, but not now.

Different Circumstances

Homeowner #1: This fits many of my subscribers. This person's home is free and clear of any mortgages. He is not using it as a "piggy bank" to borrow for consumer spending. He believes his posterity should make their own wealth and is not that concerned with leaving a major asset in his estate. He believes the current market value of his home is an irrelevance because it has no practical impact in his life. It's his paid-for castle and safe haven as long as he lives.

Solution? He should probably do nothing, depending on his assets and income. If he has sufficient dependable income and doesn't need to tap his home piggy bank, then the ups and downs of the real estate market, even over a period of several years, is a total irrelevance to him and he shouldn't concern himself with what his house is worth at any given moment. Or he could borrow against his home and invest the proceeds.

Homeowner #2: This man has a small mortgage balance and a large home equity, and his equity is a major element in his wealth analysis. This person must consider several factors. If he is concerned about the assault on his overall wealth occasioned by the collapsing real estate market, then he needs to take any one of several steps to preserve his wealth and redirect it into inflation hedges.

If he has an ARM (adjustable-rate mortgage) and limited income, he should worry about increases in his monthly payout as his monthly payment resets. And the adjustable rate means that in a rising interest-rate environment, it will only reset upward! If his other resources and income won't permit him to deal with it, or if he just plain doesn't like what's happening, he can do several things:

He can (and should) convert his ARM (if he has one) into a fixed-rate mortgage. That way his cash outlay is fixed for the foreseeable future as interest rates rise. This is not an exciting strategy if interest rates don't rise. In fact if they remain stable or decline, he would be a loser, as he would have locked in a higher interest rate than he would have paid with his ARM. But if your assumption is that interest rates and inflation will rise, this is exactly the right thing to do.

Some feel that interest rates will fall because the collapsing residential real estate market and subsequent recession will cause the Fed to lower rates to stimulate the economy. But many other factors determine interest rates. It's not just the Fed; there is a huge international free market for dollars (trillions), and the dollars have a price—interest rates! Many factors can control the perceived value of the dollar. If the dollar is losing value against other currencies (like now), then central-bank foreign holders of dollars (billions) might be tempted to switch and look for higher returns (gold) or stronger currencies. This could be very good for gold and silver and maybe some foreign currency markets, but the Fed will raise interest rates to strengthen the dollar so foreigners (particularly China and Japan) may be more inclined to keep their money (hundreds of billions) in the world's biggest currency—the dollar, via Treasury debt—in the pursuit of higher yields.

The Fed will have to think long and hard before lowering interest rates for domestic purposes because of its massive impact on the dollar, as money in the international markets tends to chase yields. If yields fall, the dollar will fall.

Interest rates will have to rise because of foreign holders of Treasury securities, further hurting real estate.

I heard many of these same arguments in favor of lower interest rates during the seventies, while interest rates were soaring to a peak of 18%, and we made a bundle in safe money-market funds, which was a relatively new investment idea. Many of my subscribers earned as much as 18% a year for a few years. But the argument was that interest rates would have to be lowered to stimulate the economy, but the foreign imperative won out. Foreign holdings of U.S. government securities are vastly greater now than in the seventies. The Fed has even more incentive to increase rates now than it did then.

If, however, you believe interest rates will remain stable or fall, then you don't want to convert to a fixed-rate mortgage or borrow against your equity.

Homeowner #3: He believes that interest rates will rise, that home prices will continue to fall, and he is concerned about this attack on his wealth, either because he wants to leave a bigger estate for his offspring or he is just concerned with the value of a major part of his wealth. If he has this outlook on his home value, then he will want to take steps to protect it. My strategy of borrowing against the equity and putting the money to work should be attractive to him, and it is precisely the right thing for him to do.

Right now, you may pay more interest on the mortgage than you will earn investing. If you have taken the equity out of your home and real estate prices drop, which they are doing now and will continue to do for a few years, then you can look at your personal balance sheet and realize that your equity has not shrunk if you have detached it from your home. One aggressive variation is to simply put at least some of the money into gold or silver, preferably a silver ETF, and turn your equity into a growing asset. If you think I'm right about precious metals and you are concerned with increasing your wealth rather than seeing it shrink and have an abundance of guts, you might want to consider this strategy.

Homeowner #4: He has bought my scenario and believes that interest rates will rise and home equities will be savaged by the sick real estate market.

Your strategy would vary. One important factor is the stability of your income. You do have to service the mortgage every month. Many people depend on the monthly proceeds from an underfunded pension. Right now there is an epidemic of them. Sooner or later, underfunded pensions will have to be cut or even eliminated. If your income is dependent upon such a pension, then I would worry about even being able to service the mortgage debt out of your income. That could be solved by simply using some of the proceeds of your loan to make your monthly payments. That means your principal will shrink by the amount of your monthly payments, but the monthly payments would give you tax benefits, which need to be cranked into the equation, and ensure that your net worth is increasing as the principal is paid down each month.

So one size does not fit all. You have to look at your own personal circumstances. The one thing that is very sure is that if you don't agree with my scenario of falling real estate prices and rising interest rates, the strategy I have been talking about is not appropriate for you.

The Sure Deal

There is, of course, one sure way to deal with falling real estate prices. You can sell the home now, realize the profits, and put this money to work in whatever way you want. Then you can rent a nice place somewhere. That way you have frozen your equity for all time to come because you don't even own the house anymore. Yogi Berra once said, "Forecasting is hard, especially if it's about the future." We are in a difficult time where you just can't stand still unless the outcome is irrelevant to you. It depends on your income, its stability, and your other assets.

Basically, you have to evaluate this for yourself because everyone's circumstances are so different. But bet on this: Home real estate prices will continue to drop, interest rates will rise in the long term along with ARM rates, and precious metals will go up, up, up!

No Debt?

I have received some e-mails from a few Latter-day Saint (Mormon) subscribers who are concerned about my advice because our church leaders have counseled us against going into debt. So is borrowing against your property a good or bad idea? A lot depends on what you do with the proceeds. Debt is not the evil; spending is the evil to be avoided.

If you borrow against your home and put the proceeds into a bigger home than you need, or buy an entertainment center, an extra car, or a newer, bigger, better one, that is a problem. But if you put the proceeds into productive assets that over the life of the loan will produce more than they cost, that's okay. You do have a small risk on the downside if the assets don't go in the direction you thought.

If you borrow against your home and put the money into a money-market fund, then it is good because the increased debt is offset by the proceeds of the money-market fund, so you could pay off the new mortgage anytime you wish if you decide things aren't going the direction you thought. If the assets go the wrong way, the small losses are basically an insurance premium against the downside. It is a relatively small price to pay as an insurance premium against risk.

Real estate is one of the great puzzles of our time. The two biggest financial areas to be concerned about today are: dropping real estate prices and rising precious metals. Gold and silver will be somewhat worrisome from time to time, even in a long-term bull market, as they can be very static or even downhill for a year or two at a time. That was also true in the seventies, but those who had patience and bought on the dips made lots of money before gold peaked out at $900 and silver at $50.

The falling real estate market that I forecast is now here for sure. Bet on falling real estate prices unless it just plain doesn't matter to you.

* * *

Real estate is a frequently requested subject in *The Ruff Times*, because it touches more people's lives than any form of money deployment. At this point I only want to discuss the home you live in, and touch on some general investment principles. Here I'll limit myself to an analysis of what the future holds for your home.

Taking My Own Advice: A Prophecy Fulfilled

A recent study by Walter X. Burns and Charles D. Kirkpatrick, of the marketing forecasting division of Lynch, Jones & Ryan, came to the same conclusion. They said that the mania in housing prices was nearing its peak, and the outlook was for a "humpty-dumpty crash in the immediate future."

When asked how bad it might be, they said, the decline might match the 80% drop in stock prices that followed the crash of 1929.

I agree, insofar as the expensive suburbs and the cities are concerned. The crash is now history in the making. As the financial panic develops, most of the troubles will be concentrated in the big cities. When it is over, there will be some tremendous bargains and you may want to come back someday. But in the meantime, I would prefer to observe from a distance.

12

WHY WALL STREET HATES GOLD AND SILVER

Wall Street ignored gold and silver during most of the 1970s hyperprofitable bull market. They were either outright hostile, or acted as though the metals didn't even exist. I got no respect, even though the first edition of this book sold 2.6 million copies and was near or at the top of the *New York Times* bestseller list in both hard and softcover for two years, and I was all over the media: *Wall Street Week*, *Oprah* twice, *Regis and Kathy Lee* three times, and more. They were usually hostile also. Wall Street paid little attention to gold until it reached about $650, far too late for them to have much of a chance for their clients to make money. In retrospect, we know that in 1979 the aging bull market was about to expire, which it did soon after when it made a brief climactic spurt to $850, and then went into a multiyear decline. They did their usual thing; they bought high, and then held on too long and sold low.

Why the hostility? Partly because they believed their own rhetoric. Historically, because rising gold always means falling stocks or a troubled world, and they made most of their commissions in the stock market, they had to remain bullish on stocks and bearish on gold. Their bullish stock market recommendation was necessary because investors wouldn't buy stocks if their advisers were dubious about the market's future. They sneered at the inflation fears of us gold and silver fans, and derisively called gold investors "gold bugs." I didn't get any respect from Wall Street and didn't expect any, even despite my book's success. That's OK, because I have lost much of my respect for them, also for a lot of reasons. I also didn't get any apologies from any of them when inflation rose to 18% and gold went to $850 and silver to $50, and didn't expect any. Unfortunately, most of the young whipper-snappers who now control Wall Street were in diapers 25 to 30 years ago during the last gold bull market, so they haven't experienced rising gold and inflation. Consequently, another gold bull market is inconceivable to them.

Studying Psychoceramics

I can't resist telling you about one of the funniest things that ever happened to me that illustrates the skepticism of mainstream media types regarding gold and silver. In 1978, I was on a national promotion tour for the first edition of this book when I found myself in Detroit, rushing to a TV station for a scheduled interview on a big morning show. I barely got there in time when the red light on the camera turned on. The host turned to the camera and said, "Today we're going to study psychoceramics, and with us today is a crackpot from California." And the interview went downhill from there, his biggest argument being that silver was an impractical investment for most people unless you were very rich.

One year later I found myself in the same studio, same host, promoting the mass paperback of my book. But this time when the light went on, he said, "Today we have with us one of America's most brilliant financial advisers," and the interview was terrific from then. After the show, I reminded him of what he had said before, and asked him what had changed his mind. He very sheepishly said, "I read your book and bought silver from a local coin dealer, and tripled my money since you were here last." So the media is not always infallible, even though they are usually wrong.

Inside Wall Street

Let me explain to you how Wall Street works. It is a culture, as well as a financial institution.

Most of the young brokers who are the big producers on Wall Street are college graduates who have been trained in the stock market. In order to get the necessary advanced licenses to work there, they are trained in all the conventional investment vehicles and their relevant laws and regulations. Then they build their clientele based on the stock market. Commissions are how they make their money.

But they are all human beings after all, subject to all the errors of habit and behavior and peer pressure that plague all of us. They are surrounded by "group-think." They make tons of money on the status quo. I have visited firms on Wall Street with big trading rooms full of twenty-something men and women whose annual income is measured in the millions—all in commissions on stock sales.

Few big Wall Street firms sell bullion (right offhand I can't think of any, although the ETFs will probably change that), so it is only money out of their pockets if hotshot brokers tell their clients to sell some stock and put the money into bullion or coins. Maturity and client concern are scarce commodities on Wall Street.

If you could meet these young brokers, you would be astounded at how money-oriented they are. They talk about their commissions and the things they buy with them. In their parking garage, I never saw so many Porsches and Lexuses and Mercedeses. Too many of them are bloodless mercenaries. And they are congenitally bullish on stocks, because that's where their bread is buttered.

Jim Dines is a case in point. At one time he was Wall Street's fair-haired boy. He wrote a book on technical investment analysis that is still a classic, and his studies told him that we were moving into a giant gold bull market. Not being very reticent by nature, he made no secret of what he had concluded, and he went from fair-haired boy to outcast. It wasn't long until he and Wall Street had to part ways. But Jim is the very definition of "maverick," so he started perhaps one of the first gold newsletters and called himself "the Original Gold Bug." He was there before me. Jim and I became friends, and he was even a guest on my TV show, *Ruffhou$e*. I honor him as a real pioneer and thank Wall Street for firing him. The newsletter business would be poorer without him, and he is still publishing, and he is well worth reading (see Appendix A). He has a quirky life and is one of the bigger egos in a business that is loaded with big egos (like me), but he is a true professional, and an example of how Wall Street is so antigold.

Financial Shows

Many of you listen to or watch financial shows. They are populated with guests who are typical examples of mainstream Wall Street financial thinking. The hosts and hostesses of the shows are steeped in the same traditions and attitudes. On the rare occasions when I am asked to be on such a show, I know that the hosts are either ignorant of my real financial views or are spoiling for a fight. Until gold and silver have risen so far they can't ignore them any longer, they will not be interested in guys like me. Until then, we gold and silver investors will be operating in what amounts to an open underground movement, below the radar.

If your broker's opinion is important to you, you may be uncomfortable here. If you aren't a maverick, you had better become one, and be quiet about it. You will have to leave the herd, and for a while, the herd is all on Wall Street.

Gold, Silver, and the Perfect Storm

Gold and silver can be useful in both a "best case" and a "worst case" set of circumstances. Both of them will be immensely profitable in very different ways, and the outlook is very different. First let's investigate . . .

THE WORST CASES: TERRORISM AND OTHER THINGS

The worst case is easy to describe. It means that terrible things have changed the very nature of America and the world. Let's consider just a few of the possible scenarios.

Remember that 95% of the dollars in existence are in cyberspace—in the computers of banks. The terrorists have enough money to hire the best hackers in the world, and there is no computer system in the world that can't be hacked into, given enough time, money, and talent. Where could Osama bin Laden get the most bang for the buck? By destroying or corrupting the computers that run the monetary system of the Western world.

He already attempted to do just that when he brought down the World Trade Center. Fortunately, his intelligence was out of date. Until about a year earlier many of those computers that control the monetary system of the world had been in the World Trade Center, but they were recently moved across the Hudson River to New Jersey, as well as to Panama. Consequently, rather than the dollar and the Western (Christian) world's currency and bond markets being destroyed by the hideous blow, the markets were up and running in a very few days with hardly a burp. But there is an even more deadly and less risky alternative for bin Laden.

PANAMA AND THE DOLLAR

When we negotiated away the Panama Canal to Omar Torrijos, the Panamanian dictator, our chief negotiator was Sol Linowitz, a member of the board of Chemical Bank in New York. He was appointed to serve for one day less than six months, so his appointment would not be subject to congressional approval, and sure enough, the giveaway deal was signed one day before Linowitz's term was up.

One key part of Linowitz's banker-inspired mission was that the Canal Zone would be a "free-banking zone," not subject to regulations or oversight. Even before the deal was signed, bank buildings were going up all over the Zone. Every multinational bank was there, and it appears that they moved many of their international money systems there, with no oversight or regulation. Who is there to determine their safety or vulnerability? No one.

If terrorist hackers were to hack into those computers and infect them with a destructive virus, the entire dollar-based monetary system would disappear in a nanosecond. In that case, for all practical purposes, the only spendable money left would be gold or silver coins or barter in a disrupted world.

And what if they were able to sneak a nuke onto a ship and detonate it while in the Canal? It's already bad enough that the Chinese are in control of the ports on both ends of the canal. Imagine the chaos with the banks obliterated and commerce fatally crippled.

Or maybe they would only hack into the air traffic control system, indefinitely grounding every commercial plane in America, or into the North American power grid, and your ATM or the electronically operated cash registers at the supermarket wouldn't work and the stores couldn't open, and food in the freezers would slowly thaw and spoil. Wouldn't it be ironic if the monetary system of the world was brought down by some idiot/savant of a seventeen-year-old al-Qaeda-paid genius or hacker, driven by money, ego, and political ignorance?

Or what if terrorists manage to smuggle a nuclear weapon into the U.S. and detonate it, taking out the government, the

Pentagon, or a few million people, throwing America into chaos, and driving gold and silver into the stratosphere. Or explode nuclear weapons in the stratosphere, destroying every transistor within hundreds of miles with an EMP (electromagnetic pulse).

These and innumerable other scenarios may seem beyond the edges of credibility, but I dare you to say they are not possible. And I am sure there are other scenarios I haven't thought of yet. This is not a forecast, only a speculation about a possible worst-case, we-hope-not, scenario.

THE HYPERINFLATION SCENARIO

What if monetary inflation rises as a result of soaring demands on government with its soaring deficits, and subsequent, inevitable consumer inflation rises until defensive consumer buying breaks out into a real hyperinflation, with the modern money machine running night and day, like Germany during the 1920s. This would make money increasingly worthless and precious metals increasingly precious. History tells us that this has happened over and over again, and we are repeating most of the same deadly mistakes today.

Let's pretend we are transported into a future where America is devastated by hyperinflation, and see what it looks like.

The world will be in terrible trouble, and the prosperity and comfort that now surround you will be in tatters. You will be surrounded by people struggling to survive, let alone prosper, as in the 1930s. That's what happened in Germany after the hyperinflation of the deutsche mark, and this general suffering was the fertile ground that gave birth to Adolf Hitler, dictator. If you prospered by holding gold and silver, you could buy a lot of safety and security while the country is being mended.

These are only a few of the possibilities. You can probably come up with better ones than I did. Share them with me, but don't give up hope. There is still . . .

THE BEST CASE

Even if none of the worst-case scenarios ever happens, and we wipe out or neutralize al-Qaeda and the currency system hangs together, monetary inflation has already been cooked into the economic cake by the Federal Reserve and industry, and so has the silver supply/demand situation. It is inconceivable to me, given thirty-one years of studying and monitoring the economics of inflation, that the flood of "money" being poured into the economy of the world will not result in a ruinous inflation. If that doesn't happen, we will be making history; it will be the first time that the money machines have run out of control and the result was not a ruinous, big-time inflation. Even in this "best-case" situation, you will make a bundle on this monetary-inflation-sensitive investment, even in a still orderly world.

If all else fails, you can count on Social Security, Medicare, and the prescription drug program to trigger a flood of "money printing" in the trillions of dollars, with subsequent monetary inflation following this as night follows the day. As it becomes obvious to the public that these programs are plummeting into insolvency, the consumer inflation rate will soar, and so will gold and silver.

When the dire facts become obvious, Congress will start desperately searching for solutions, but which ones? Will they raise taxes and watch FICA soar and taxpayers revolt?

I doubt it. Will they cut benefits or raise the Social Security retirement age? Maybe a little bit, but not much. Will they dig in their heels and memorialize the current dysfunctional system by simply printing money? You bet! This will lay the groundwork for more ruinous inflation, and soaring gold and silver.

In this best case (the most likely—I think), we will at least see rising inflation and an inflationary recession (which is already written in stone), and gold and silver and the metals and their mining stocks will go up—perhaps five to ten times, perhaps a lot more.

There is no best-case—or worst-case—scenario in which I can conceive of gold and silver being losers. You can mortgage the kids and bet the farm! We can keep the odds decisively on our side!

13

EARNING INCOME IN AN AGE OF INFLATION

Many of my readers are retired or widowed and need regular income from their investments. How can you get income when you have bought into my vision and converted your savings into gold and silver for capital gains, rather than bonds, utility stocks, or dividend-paying stocks for income, all of which will be less and less viable in an age of inflation (do the math)?

The usual "conservative" financial-adviser counsel for retired older people is to buy bonds, utility stocks, or dividend-paying blue-chip stocks. In fact, now that many Wall Street advisers are now worried about the immediate future of the stock market, especially "growth stocks," they are going back to the old standby, "shift more of your holdings into more conservative investments," like bonds.

Here is an oddball idea that flies in the face of conventional wisdom. Buy gold and ETFs and sell off say 8%, or whatever you need, of your shares each year for income. This strategy has several advantages. If I am right about the bull market in the metals, the remaining shares will appreciate faster than your withdrawal. Your capital will keep growing.

No, No, No! Bad Choices!

Bonds are an especially bad idea in a time of rising inflation and interest rates, and they will be rising for the foreseeable future. But why are bonds such a bad idea?

- You shouldn't lock yourself into low bond yields when rates are rising, which they *always* do in the long term when inflation is rising. If you do, in the future you will look with envy on those who waited and are getting higher rates.

- When interest rates rise, the market value of bonds goes down, and that is also true of any fixed-return investment. What you gain in income will be more than offset by capital losses. In the seventies, I watched as interest rates and money-market fund yields climbed above 18%, and bonds (even supersafe T-bonds) lost up to half of their market value, and so did dividend-paying utility stocks.

So what's to be done? There are several alternatives, some of them very unorthodox, and some are only for the future.

Yes, Yes, Yes! Good Choices!

Buy shares of a money-market fund for future income as rates rise. Money-market funds are mutual funds that invest strictly in short-term securities, like short-term Treasury bills that mature in as little as a month or less. Sometimes they even buy overnight banknotes. The fund managers will turn over their whole portfolio in two or three months or less, reinvesting them at higher yields as interest rates rise. The law requires that they pass on the yields to you, and maintain shares at the same price. They are as close to being riskless as you can find in this risky world.

In the seventies, I was one of the first to advise and teach my followers about these newfangled money-market funds, as few people had even heard of them and few advisers were paying attention to them, except as temporary parking places for money that was in between other investments.

The neat thing is that you can withdraw your funds at any time by simply writing a check against them. You get the high yield of a bank CD with the liquidity of a low-yield, or no-yield, checking account. In the seventies, interest rates rose to as high as 18%, and the yield on the money-market fund I recommended did accordingly. The same thing should happen in this inflationary age. Rates are low now as this is written, but they will rise. They always do when inflation is the order of the day.

Use your money-market fund for large transactions by writing checks against it, rather than a no-yield to low-yield bank checking account. Don't get sucked into a bank "money-market account." They are the banks' reaction to the competition of legitimate money-market funds. They are not the same. They are merely bank deposits competing badly with higher yields than they used to pay before they were forced to compete. They are usually just CDs masquerading as money-market funds, complete with the deceptive label.

When money-market funds first burst upon the scene in the late seventies, bankers considered them a serious threat. They already had lobbied for and gotten Regulation Q, which, in effect (and conveniently), prevented them from raising interest rates for demand depositors. These accounts were limited by law to very, very low interest rates. Small savers were saving their liquid money in low-yielding passbook accounts rather than tying up their money for months in high-yielding CDs, and the banks were loaning out the money very profitably by issuing CDs or making mortgage loans at much higher interest rates.

Shortly after we moved to Utah, I found myself in the middle of a fight to the death between the banking industry and the money-market funds. There was a bill before the state legislature that had already passed the Upper House, and seemed to be a slam dunk in the Lower House. It was very deceptive because it would require money-market funds to set aside the same cash reserves banks had to set aside, forcing them to lower their interest yields to say alive. It would also have driven money-market funds out of the state of Utah, as federal law would not permit the funds to discriminate by states, and they had no such pressure in the other forty-nine states.

I got a call from a representative of the mutual-fund industry who asked me to use my influence on state legislators (assuming I had such) to help kill the bill. I agreed because I realized it was simply an anticompetitive attack by the banks. I prepared an article for *The Ruff Times* and had copies placed on every legislator's desk the night before the final vote. I was asked to be the last speaker before "the conference of the whole," meaning the whole legislature. When I arrived at the State Capitol and went to the chamber room, I saw the galleries full of bankers from every small town in Utah glaring at their legislative constituents on the floor.

A week before this, I had gotten a call from Ezra Taft Benson, former secretary of agriculture, who was a close friend and also president of the Quorum of the Twelve Apostles of the LDS Church and a later church president. He had read my *Ruff Times* article on the subject, and he asked me to meet with the president of the Utah Bankers Association because "they have explained this bill to me," and he wanted me to listen.

In today's political environment with the Romney candidacy, a lot of people are unjustifiably worried that Mormon elected officials will sometimes be forced to travel in lockstep as the church wants them to. This was a test of those alleged fears. I had breakfast with Elder Benson's banker friend and was unconvinced, and so reported to Elder Benson. He said to me, "Thank you for listening and thanks for caring." So I got ready to lecture these legislators against this anticompetitive bill.

I was the last speaker. The room was full of electricity as I stood at the rostrum. I argued that this was an anticompetitive bill sponsored by a competitive industry group, and many of the legislators had been swept into office on the basis of the Reagan revolution, whose free market principles were in direct contradiction.

After I spoke, and before the final vote, there was a recess. I went to the cloakroom to wait. While I was there, one legislator, who was the son of an LDS general authority and was the floor leader for the bankers, cornered me to argue. He is a nice fellow, but he was just plain wrong, and he was accompanied by about five of his legislator friends who listened very intently to the discussion. Shortly after this, the legislature voted. Four of the five men who were with us changed their votes, and the bill was defeated by four votes, rather than being passed by five as everyone expected.

Radio, TV, and print reporters were swarming all over the place trying to figure out how the expected outcome had been changed. They were interviewing people right and left, totally ignoring me. At the time, I had not yet achieved the notoriety I would have over the next few years, so as far as they were concerned, I was invisible. But we prevented the money-market funds from being driven out of the state of Utah, which would have given Utah bankers free reign.

Partly as a result of this and partly as the national success of this new investment medium nationwide, the bankers lobbied to eliminate Regulation Q, as they now could compete and offer higher interest rates on liquid accounts to compete with the money-market funds, which is now the case. Regulation Q had been driving investors into higher-yielding CDs, which would lock up the money for months for the bankers to use, and they could still make a nice but smaller profit loaning it out at higher rates. Small savers were no longer locked into infinitesimal yields on "passbook accounts" and no-yield checking accounts, and money-market funds became the worthy competitor they are today.

Another Good Choice

Canadian oil and gas funds have been paying 9 to 15% annually. With the soaring price of crude oil, natural gas, and gas at the pump, these high yields should continue into the foreseeable future. Under Canadian tax laws, as these funds invest in oil and gas production, which is what they do, if they pay out most of their income (over 95%) as dividends, they are not taxed at the fund level, so there is no double taxation like with other corporations, cutting into their dividend yields. So savers needing or wanting high yields have swarmed to them.

Recently the Canadian government (like all tax-hungry, predatory governments) announced they would start taxing them. But the resulting investor uproar caused them to modify the proposal, so they announced that when, and if, they taxed them, they would exempt the funds already in existence before that date and "grandfather" them for four years. Of course, that has cut off the development of new funds. Most of these older funds still have high yields.

These stocks have several advantages as the price of oil climbs, which it will. Not only will the dividend increase with rising oil prices, but the stocks will also go up with rising oil, and the dividend will increase as the subsequent rising profits are passed on to you. Here is a partial list; there are several other acceptable ones.

Advantage Energy Income Fund (AVN.UN-T) yielding 14.6%; Baytex Energy Trust (BTE.UN-T) yielding 11.2%; Enerplus Resources Fund (ERF) yielding 11.3%; and Paramount Energy Trust (PMT.UN-T) yielding 13.9%. These trusts are designed to generate income. Approximately 1% of the yield is retained to cover expenses, and the rest is paid out as dividends to shareholders. They are a great income investment, as long as oil prices rise or even remain stable. If you believe oil prices will fall, I will cover all bets. Current yields change daily, so call Jim Raby at National Securities (800-

431-4488) for the latest quotes and his recommendations. Unlike most other brokers, who cannot buy foreign (Canadian) securities, Jim's firm can, so he is a great source. That's true also of many mining stocks. I have no financial interest in your transactions with Raby. You're welcome.

There is also one other possibility in the future. Gold and silver-mining stocks, as they soar, may find themselves with more cash than they know what to do with from profitable mining. They may pay big dividends in the future. They now pay only nominal ones.

You can get more information from my most recent book, *Ruff's Little Book of Big Fortunes in Gold and Silver* or from *The Ruff Times*. You can access these at www.rufftimes2.com.

14

COLLECT YOUR INSURANCE BEFORE YOU DIE

A new industry has turned into a big business. That is the purchasing of existing life insurance policy death benefits, which insure seniors over sixty-five, by large financial institutions and investment funds. Several large financial institutions will purchase existing seniors' life insurance policies for more than the cash value. They will even buy term-life insurance policies that have no cash value, if the term policy still has the right to convert to a permanent policy.

Blair Whiting first brought this to my attention, and I asked him to write an article about it for *The Ruff Times*. I have worked with Blair for many years on insurance needs. Since then, I also got a letter on the same subject from Irving L. Blackman, chairman of the board of a Chicago community bank, but who still consults for estate planning.

This new idea works like this:

Joe, 69 years old, owns a life insurance policy with a $500,000 death benefit and a $65,000 cash surrender value, and he wants to stop paying premiums because he doesn't need so much insurance. Typically he would cancel the policy and get the $65,000 cash from the insurance company.

Instead, an investor (or a group of investors—many financial institutions, banks, and hedge funds are all now purchasing these policies) buys Joe's policy for $150,000, paid in cash to Joe immediately. The investors now own the policy and will receive the $500,000 death benefit when Joe dies.

This proposal is limited to older readers (over 65, some major financial institutions have gone down to age 60), so the investor won't have to wait too long until you kick the bucket, and the purchase of the life insurance policy is a real windfall for everyone. The buyer of your policy assumes he can collect the full face value when you die, and you can get a good piece of that face value *before* you die. It's a win/win situation (except for the fact, of course, that you're dead).

You can learn more about this by contacting Blair Whiting at 800-441-5611, or e-mail him at bwhiting@sfs.nfp.com.

Once you've cashed in that policy, you can put the cash to work in the investments I am recommending in this book or, if you're not persuaded, you can put it in the investment of your choice. That can give you an operating investment fund, and you no longer have to make premium payments, which can help your cash flow. That cash can be put into investments or survival preparations instead of premiums.

There is also a way to be one of the investors who cash in on this sure thing. You invest $100,000 and wind up with a diversified portfolio of purchased insurance policies (actually a fractional interest in several of these policies).

Let's review.

1. If you have a life insurance policy you no longer want or need, don't just stop paying the premiums and drop the policy. The policy should be appraised to see what it is actually worth. In many cases it can be worth much more than just the cash value. For example, let's assume an insured senior, age seventy-two, has a life insurance policy with a death benefit of $500,000. Let's also assume the policy has a $20,000 cash value. If the policy is no longer needed, then you can use the old traditional method to cash in the policy for the $20,000 cash value.

But there is a better way that can produce much more cash. You can get an appraisal on the policy and make the policy available for sale on the senior life-settlement market, where a cash payment of $30,000 to possibly as high as $200,000 may be realized for that type of policy. The amount paid for the policy will vary depending on the insured's health, age, the type of policy, and other factors. But, if a financial institution is interested in buying your policy, the purchase price will always be more than your cash value. Perhaps some life insurance coverage is still needed, just not as much.

2. You could sell part of the policy. For example, again assuming a $500,000 death benefit, a life-settlement company might be willing to buy part of the death benefit (maybe for $300,000), pay all of the premiums, and when the insured passes away, still pay $200,000 to the insured's beneficiaries.

3. This strategy can be an excellent way to reduce the amount of premium outlay for needed life insurance coverage.

Some Cautions

If you sell all or part of your life insurance policy, it will still count against how much insurance you can qualify for, based on your financial situation. The average Joe knows you have to qualify for life insurance policies based on your health. But, many people don't realize that you also have to qualify based on your net worth and income. The amount of life insurance you can qualify for is called "capacity." It is a good idea to have your financial adviser give you a feel for your life insurance capacity before you consider selling your old life insurance policy.

In addition, get full disclosure as to commissions and look at all bids. Commissions can vary dramatically in this industry. Depending on the amount of work for the financial adviser/broker, a fair commission is usually between 2 to 4% of your death benefit.

If the required criteria are met and it is a round peg in a round hole, it can still help you meet your life insurance objectives. If you're interested, give Blair Whiting a call at 800-441-5611.

If you are interested in being one of an investment group who buys these policies, which is a lead-pipe cinch to make 15 to 20% on every deal, you can fax Irving L. Blackman at 847-674-5299 with your name, address, and phone numbers. You must be an accredited investor, and the minimum investment is $50,000.

15

"DO THY PATIENT NO HARM"

I have tried to follow the admonition of Hippocrates to the new physician, to give you advice that will not hurt you if either my forecast or my timetable is wrong. You also need to know now how to switch strategies if the tide should change.

It's now time to put all this advice together in one easy summation so you can come up with a personal program that fits your life and personal perspective.

First, I'd like to deal with one important principle we have not tackled thus far. It's important in the overall scheme of things. Most of you cannot go heavily now into gold and silver because you need liquid cash. Your survival efforts (part II) should be completed now, but we all need to have some liquid funds to maintain an orderly financial life while things are relatively normal. I have exactly the same question to answer: What do I do with those liquid funds when I am nervous about the banking system?

There are two acceptable alternatives. You can invest in either Treasury bills or in money-market funds.

T-bills are the shortest-term obligations of the U.S. government, with maturities generally between 90 and 120 days. They are "discount instruments," which means they sell at a discount from their face value and are cashed in at their face value at maturity, and the difference between the price-when-issued and the face value at maturity represents your interest return. T-bills generally are in $10,000 denominations, so you can't play that game unless you can buy in big chunks. In fact, a "round lot" in the T-bill market is $1 million, and you don't get the best price unless you buy them in round lots. The longer the maturity, the larger the market risk.

The advantage of Treasury bills is that their maturities are so short that if interest rates rise, you don't suffer a market loss. You merely wait three or four months until they mature and cash in at the face value, plus accumulated interest. If interest rates were to rise abruptly and you had to liquidate suddenly, they might drop a little in market value. In a period of rising interest rates, smart money managers "go short," which in the money market means they convert all their holdings into the shortest-term securities, and Treasury bills fit that need.

You can buy shares of money-market funds that invest in Treasury bills or other very short-term money-market instruments, especially if you don't have enough money to buy T-bills in $10,000 increments.

A government-securities money-market fund is a no-load mutual fund that invests strictly in U.S. short-term securities. You buy their shares, on which no commission is charged (no-load) as you deal directly with the company and no salesman is involved, and they invest the money in T-bills. The earned profit is passed on to you, although the management does extract a fee of one-half of 1% of the total assets. But because they buy in $1 million round lots, they are able to buy the T-bills for less money than you could, and that generally covers the management fees. The rate of return on the fund should be very close to that of the prevailing T-bill rate. You can take your money out at any time. Even better, they issue you blank checks on their bank, and you can write checks against your T-bill account as though it were an interest-bearing checking account, as long as each check is over $250.

The money-market fund check-writing privilege is used by many corporate financial managers. It's a parking place for funds that are waiting to be deployed otherwise, or which are necessary for business or personal liquidity.

There are other money-market funds that utilize the same principle, but earn higher yields because they buy commercial paper, bank paper, and other short-term debt obligations, which earn more than T-bills but with somewhat less safety. It does not offer quite the same range of security as a T-bill fund, but the higher yield makes it worth your consideration. They also offer check-writing privileges.

One reason I am quite enamored of T-bills is that in a real financial panic there is an instinctive flow of money in two directions: 1) toward gold and silver; and 2) toward Uncle Sam. During the Depression of the thirties, when banks were going broke, government securities were the hot item, and they were actually bid up so high that they delivered negative yields. When everything is coming down around your ears, you want your liquid money in the thing that is likely to come down last so you have a chance to make a move. The T-bill is your hedge against being caught without sufficient time to act. There is a huge market for T-bills and they can be bought and sold at any time. Their liquidity advantage, plus interest, plus check-writing privileges, make money-market funds the ideal parking place for unemployed money.

I like to have liquid cash equal to six-month installment obligations. Having those funds in T-bills or a money-market fund is the equivalent of keeping them in cash.

For Instance

Now after you have met your liquidity requirements, let's take a look at some sample portfolios for a family of three, each with $10,000, $50,000, or $100,000 to invest during a period of rising inflation and interest rates.

You must understand the present, accurately perceive the future, have a plan that doesn't violate the principles of this book, and be willing to move in whatever direction the intermediate changes in our economic course should indicate while maintaining your stable always-in-place survival position. Prepare for inflation, but be ready to catch any major interruption in the inflationary trend with the break-even-or-better strategy, moving between bonds and gold.

You might buy and read this book at some time in the future when we have moved from an inflationary upward move into a prolonged deflationary correction with falling interest rates. In that case, you would substitute bonds for your holdings of gold and silver. What is important is that you understand the principles so the answers come naturally when the tide changes.

My biggest problem in setting guidelines for you is to teach you how to recognize the signals of the changing tide. It's pretty easy in the abstract to say, "Interest rates are falling, buy bonds," or, "Interest rates are going up, buy gold." How do you tell the difference between a short-term move and a long-term trend? Basically you can't unless you spend a lot of time watching, as I do. And there I hope *The Ruff Times* (www.rufftimes2.com) can be helpful. In all honesty, it's not absolutely necessary to your well-being to be a *Ruff Times* subscriber if you really have mastered the principles of this book, but it could be pretty helpful.

There are some things developing in the world that might shoot down all my options. For example, if the Russians continue building their aggressive missile program and their war machine, or if nuclear war breaks out between the Russians and the Chinese, or if Iran nukes Tel Aviv, or there is another big terrorist attack here, then we face a confused economic environment that no one can really understand. In that case, you go for the ultimate chaos-hedge with the best odds, and that's gold and food. Go all-out with everything you can scrape together.

In Paul Erdman's book *The Crash of '79*, his hero was an ex-American banker working as a financial adviser to the king of Saudi Arabia. As soon as he saw that war was about to break out in the Middle East, he immediately liquidated all of his paper holdings and bought nothing but gold, and that is precisely what you should do under those same conditions. My general attitude is to err on the side of the defensive position, and not be too anxious to catch each trend at its exact turning point. Unless it is a sudden calamity, like war, wait until a trend has been established.

Send Me a Man Who Reads

The International Paper Company once ran a great advertising campaign that said, "Send me a man who reads." A person who is not willing to read could lose everything he has when the economy moves contrary to his basic premises. I have a list of publications in Appendix A that I read for information and education.

OTHER VALUABLE SOURCES OF INFORMATION AND INVESTMENT RECOMMENDATIONS

What I Read

The Wall Street Journal: Everyone should read the *Wall Street Journal*. Its editorials are the best to be found anywhere. The statistical information regarding money supply, and markets, and some of the "think pieces" on the front and back pages are invaluable. It should be scanned every day.

When I read it, I look for the feature articles on the front page, then turn to the commodities section about two-thirds of the way through, and then hit the editorial page, especially the editorials in the left-hand column. Anyone who wants to protect his assets who does not read the *Wall Street Journal* is foolish.

Business Week, Forbes, and Fortune: I wade through all these magazines as soon as they hit my desk. *Business Week* is a very conservative, somewhat sober, but generally quite accurate analysis of what's going on in the world. I have found a lot of key pieces of data from which very important decisions have been made.

Forbes: Even though it has been wrong in many of its editorial conclusions, is a useful source of data. Just ignore their generally anti–hard money stance. They declared gold dead when it was $110 an ounce, so they are not very objective about gold and silver, but it's still well worth reading.

Time, Newsweek, & U.S. News & World Report: These are the standard newsmagazines. I don't read them for opinion. I read them for information, and then I apply my own standard of judgment as to how objective they are. Their liberal bias is considerable, but sometimes I find them useful when I need to know how the liberal press thinks, and everyone should read them with appropriate skepticism.

ADVISORY NEWSLETTERS

The Ruff Times, P.O. Box 441, Orem, UT 84059; www.rufftimes2.com, $165 a year for e-mail subscribers. You can subscribe online.

Richard Russell's Dow Theory Letters. Written by a wise old pro. An indispensable source of market information. P.O. Box 1759, La Jolla, CA 92038; www.dowtheoryletter.com.

Casey Research. Doug Casey, a very savvy and entertaining writer with an encyclopedic knowledge of mines and metals. We have often tangled on values, but never on investments.

The Aden Forecast by Pamela and Mary Anne Aden. They are also old-timers, and their regular newsletter is clear and complete, technical but readable, and always right (they agree with me). They are great gals and great friends.

The Silver Investor Report by David Morgan. www.silver -investor.com.

Jay Taylor's Gold and Technology Report. Jay Taylor is a new friend with a towering reputation.

Gold Mining Stock Report by Bob Bishop. www.gold miningstockreport.com. Telephone: 925-284-1165 Fax: 925-891-9188.

The McAlvany Intelligence Advisor by Don McAlvany. www .publishersmanagement.com. A good guy and a recommended coin dealer.

The Dines Letter by Jim Dines, the original "gold (now uranium) bug." www.dinesletter.com. 800-845-8259. An old friend, and a most entertaining writer and speaker. Another must read!

Resource Opportunities by Lawrence Roulston. 877-773-7677. Dennis is sound and thorough, and he has done an article for me in *The Ruff Times* on uranium stocks.

Forecast & Strategies by Mark Skousen. www.mskousen .com. 800-777-5005.

Other Valuable Resources

INDISPENSABLE INFORMATION WEBSITES

www.rufftimes2.com. Both free articles and paid-subscription information.

www.321gold.com. Great articles on the subject. I may from time to time have an article there.

www.321energy.com. From the same source. Oil stocks and alternative-energy info.

www.kitco.com. A major recommended coin and bullion dealer, and a source of up-to-the-minute gold and silver quotes and lots of other info.

www.jsmineset.com. From Jim Sinclair, one of the old-timers, and a very successful (and rich) writer since the seventies.

www.thebullandbear.com. Great information on gold, silver, and other markets.

PRECIOUS METALS DEALERS

KITCO. www.kitco.com. 877-775-4826. 178 West Service Road, Champion, NY 12919. My regular source of up-to-the-minute gold and silver quotes.

Investment Rarities Inc. www.investmentrarities.com. 800-328-1860. 7850 Metro Highway, Minneapolis, MN 55425. Friends for thirty years.

International Collectors Associates. www.mcalvany.com. 800-525-9556. 166 Turner Drive, Durango, CO 81303. McAlvany is a really good guy.

Camino Coin. www.camino.com. 800-348-8001. 851 Burlway, Suite 202, Burlingame, CA 94010.

FOOD STORAGE

Preparedness Plus (800-588-5412). www.preparednessplus .net.

Martens Health and Survival (800-824-7861). www.marten survival.com.

Emergency Essentials (800-999-1863). www.beprepared .com

Karen Varner (801) 225-0948.

SURVIVAL AND TECHNOLOGY

Boy Scout Manual. Great reference material on basic survival skills. Available from any local store that sells Boy Scout supplies.

Making the Best of Basics: Family Preparedness Handbook by James Talmage Stevens. This is the bestselling book ever on basic storage programs for everyday necessities. Available in most bookstores.

Don't Get Caught with Your Pantry Down by James Talmage Stevens. Includes the most complete directory of preparedness vendors. Available in most bookstores.

Info Power III by Matthew Lesko. Available in the reference section at any good bookstore.

Websites for emergency planning: www.ready.gov and www.redcross.org. http://www.orem.org/index.php?option/ com_content&task/view&id/301&Itemid/286 is one of my local community websites that has terrific information on emergency preparation.

VITAMINS, MINERALS, AND PROTEIN

Hi-Q Nutrition. Brain Food. Manufactured by Howard Ruff (877-665-6818). On the Ruff Times website (www.rufftimes2 .com) and www.hiqnutrition.com.

Neolife. Norvel & Joann Martens (800-824-7861). I've done business with them for twenty-five years.

GOLD-MINING STOCKBROKERS

National Securities. James Raby, www.nationalsecurities .com. 800-431-4488. 1001 Fourth Avenue, 22nd Floor, Seattle, WA 98154. My broker. An honest source of info on mining stocks for his clients. Trades Canadian and U.S. stocks.

Investment Menu:
Shopping Suggestions

(This is a shopping list of recommended investments to select from, not a portfolio.)

Updates are made to this list in each issue of *The Ruff Times* (www.rufftimes2.com). Changes occur often from mergers and other activities, so please check before you buy.

INVESTING FOR INCOME

Money-market mutual funds.

Canadian oil and gas trusts: Advantage Energy Income Fund

(AVN.UN-T); **Baytex Energy Trust** (BTE.UN-T); **Enerplus Resources Fund** (ERF); **Paramount Energy Trust** (PMT.UN-T).

INVESTING FOR CAPITAL GAINS IN A BEAR MARKET

Rydex Ursa (Nasdaq: RYURX). This mutual fund is countercyclical to the S&P 500, and is great for investing in a bear market or for hedging a portfolio. It will do badly during market rallies and very well in periods of poor stock market performance.

Rydex Juno (Nasdaq: RYJUX). This mutual fund will rise when interest rates are rising, and fall when interest rates are falling. It is countercyclical to bond prices.

GOLD-MINING MUTUAL FUNDS

ASA LTD. (NYSE: ASA). A closed-end fund, owning South African mining shares. Because of the chancy political situation there, I'm cool toward it.

Central Fund of Canada Ltd. (AMEX: CEF). Listed on the American Exchange. It is a pure bullion fund and maintains a ratio of 50 ounces of silver to 1 ounce of gold. It is a near perfect proxy for bullion, which cannot often be held in an IRA or other tax-protected plan, unlike CEF.

American Century Global Gold (Nasdaq: BGEIX). An open-end, no-load mutual fund, which probably has the lowest expense ratios.

Tocqueville Gold (Nasdaq: TGLDX). An open-end, no-load mutual fund.

US Global Investors (Nasdaq: USERX): An open-end, no-load mutual fund.

Fidelity Select Gold (Nasdaq: FSAGX). An open-end fund.

ETFs (EXCHANGE-TRADED FUNDS)

The silver ETF is **iShares Silver Trust** (AMEX: SLV). The gold ETF is **Streettracks Gold Trust** (NYSE: GLD). Your shares are backed by bullion at the current price.

These gold and silver ETFs may make CEF obsolete, as you can now buy shares of each metal in whatever ratio you prefer. The gold/silver ratio may narrow to as little as 20 to 1 in the future, making silver even more profitable than gold. We will report often on the gold/silver ratio in *The Ruff Times*.

Market Vectors–Gold Miners stock ETF (GDX) is an exchange-traded fund that holds (at last count) 44 gold-mining stocks. They are the major mining stocks with broad public markets. It is a proxy for 44 of these gold and silver mining companies. It is the lazy man's way to hold a broad portfolio of these shares.

MINING STOCKS

I favor mining companies with more than 50% of production and/or properties in North America because it will reduce the political risk of expropriation. Don't ignore the other companies entirely; just make sure your portfolio is balanced toward North America. North American stocks have an asterisk in front of them.

BLUE CHIPS: MAJOR GOLD PRODUCERS

(1 million ounces annually or more)

Barrick (ABX), ***Newmont** (NYSE: NEM), **Gold Fields** (NYSE: GFI),***Goldcorp** (NYSE: GG), **Freeport McMoran**

(NYSE: FCX), *Kinross (NYSE: KGC), Anglo Gold (NYSE: AU).

SECOND-TIER PRODUCERS

(Annual production between 50,000 and 1 million ounces)

*Agnico Eagle (NYSE: AEM), *Aurizon Mines (AMEX: AZK), *Claude Resources (AMEX: CGR), Desert Sun Resources (DMS.TO), Iamgold Corp (NYSE: IAG), *Northgate (AMEX: NXG), *Yukon Nevada Gold Corp. (YNG), Yamana (AMEX: AUY).

DEVELOPMENT COMPANIES

(Mining companies that have found an ore body and are further defining it by drilling, etc. Some have proven reserves in the ground. They are often shopping for a big partner to finance their development, or even so they can sell out to them, making them acquisition candidates.)

*Alamos (AGI.TO), Arizona Star (CDNX: AZS.V), Bear Creek (CDNX: BCM.V), Continental (CDNX: KMK.V), Crystallex (AMEX: KRY), *Farallon (FAN.TO), Guyana Goldfields (GUY.TO), *Kirkland Lake (KGI.TO), Golden Star (CAMEX: GSS).

EXPLORATION COMPANIES

(The bottom of the pyramid. Looking for properties to acquire, explore, and develop. May eventually be the most profitable to own.)

Golden Arrow (CDNX: GRG.V), *US Gold (AMEX:

UXG), *Rubicon (AMEX: RBY), Madison (CDNX: MMR.V), Candente (DNT.TO), Buenaventura (NYSE: BVN), *Virginia Gold (VGQ.TO), Nevsun (AMEX: NSU), *Almaden (AMM. TO), Northern Lion (NL.V), Orezone (AMEX: OZN).

PURE SILVER MINES

(Probably the best performers of all.)

*Hecla (NYSE: HL) (a giant), Pan American Silver (Nasdaq: PAAS), *Silver Wheaton Corp. (SLW.TO), *Silver Standard Resources, Inc. (Nasdaq: SSRI), *Coeur D'Alene Mines (NYSE: CDE), *ECU Silver (CDNX: ECU.V), *Sterling (CNDX: SLG. V), *Gammon Lake (AMEX: GRS), Silvercorp Metals (SVM. TO), Endeavour Silver (CDRNX: EDR.V), Apex (AMEX: SIL).

COMBINATION PLAYS

*Northern Dynasty (AMEX: NAK)—copper and gold; Golden Star (AMEX: GSS)—gold and silver; NovaGold (AMEX: NG)—copper, gold, silver, and zinc.

URANIUM: PRODUCING COMPANIES

*Cameco (CCO.TO), Energy Resources of Australia (OTC: EGRAF.PK), Cogema unit of AREVA (OTC: ARVCF.PK), *Denison Mines (DML.TO).

JUNIOR URANIUM DEVELOPMENTS

*Strathmore Minerals (CDNX: STM.V), *Standard Uranium (CDNX: URN.V), *Energy Metals (CDNX: EMC.V), Western

Prospector (WNP: TSXV), *Crosshair Exploration (CDNX: CXX.V), CanAlaska Ventures (CDNX: CVV.V).

URANIUM EXPLORATION COMPANIES

Wealth Minerals (WML.V), *Dejour (CDNX: DJE.V).

COPPER MINING

Ivanhoe Mines (NYSE: IVN), Freeport McMoran (NYSE: FCX).

ABOUT THE AUTHOR
(BY THE AUTHOR)

If you are going to take my advice, you have every right to know what kind of a guy I am, so a little bit of history is appropriate.

Let's start with some of the fun stuff. My life has been so full and unusual that I cannot resist reprinting here something I wrote for fun a few years ago, right after a neighborhood barbecue when we played a game where we had to recount things we had done that we thought nobody else there had done. That fun trip down Memory Lane started my memory running wild. Enjoy!

* * *

- I traded one spool of eight-pound-test monofilament fishing line to a chief of a village in the Amazon jungle in return for two monkey-skull necklaces, a blow gun and darts, a bow and arrows, and an anaconda snakeskin. And, after consulting with Kay, I respectfully declined the chief's offer of a night with one of his four wives in return for a second spool.

- I've walked through the dramatic story of the death of Rasputin, the Mad Monk, right on the actual murder scene in a restored palace in Leningrad.

- I've interviewed (with Jack Anderson) newly elected President Havel of Czechoslovakia in Prague Palace while he was wearing Nike shoes and a UCLA Bruins sweatshirt. He had been a political prisoner until the Iron Curtain went down.

- I've visited the Forbidden City and the Great Wall in China, Machu Picchu, the Imperial Palace in Bangkok, wild-game preserves in Kenya and South Africa, snorkeled on the Great Barrier Reef, and watched great sea turtles lay their eggs and their baby turtles hatch.

- Ollie North, my Washington staff, and I persuaded Ronald Reagan to send Stinger missiles to the Afghan freedom fighters, which bogged down the Soviet army in Afghanistan for six years, which led to Soviet bankruptcy, which led to Gorbachev withdrawing Russian financial and military support from Eastern Europe, Cuba, and Nicaragua, which led to a breakout of freedom, which led to the crash of the Iron Curtain.

- I have sung solos with the Mormon Tabernacle Choir, the Philadelphia Orchestra, the National Symphony, and on the Ed Sullivan Show. I also performed in, conducted, or directed hundreds of performances of Gilbert and Sullivan operas and became deeply involved with the Utah Lyric Opera society as a performer, director, and general manager, and was a church choir director at age sixteen.

- I had my own national TV talk show and daily two-minute radio commentary in more than three hundred markets.

- I was called a liar in an angry speech on the floor of Congress by Congressman Neal of South Carolina, and was denounced by Pravda, Tass, and Soviet-controlled Radio Kabul as a "radical reactionary."

- I once refused a phone call from an angry President Ronald Reagan. He swore at me, and then sent me an unsolicited, personally autographed portrait as a peace offering.

- A ruffled Jimmy Carter succeeded in knocking fifty stations off my radio syndicate by threatening them with trouble at license-renewal time if they didn't cancel my show.

- I married a celestial woman, Kay. We've been through thick and thin (I used to be thin) for forty-nine years, probably because we have one thing in common: we're both in love with the same man!

- We have given birth to nine children, adopted five teenagers, and helped raise eighteen foster children—and endured the accidental death of one child.

- I broke up an orphanage run by American pedophiles in Bangkok, which resulted in jailing them and caused an international incident between ABC, me, and the Thai government. I set up my own orphanage to take care of the children in Bangkok.

- I was on *Donahue* (three times), *Good Morning America*, the *Today* show (three times), *Merv Griffin*, *Dinah Shore* (twice), *Oprah*, *Regis and Kathy Lee* (three times), *Crossfire*, *PBS Late Night*, *Nightline* (twice), *Charlie Rose*, *McNeil Lehrer*, *Wall Street Week*, and hundreds of local radio and TV talk shows, many of them multiple times.

- My 1978 edition of this book topped the bestseller lists for two years and was the biggest-selling financial book in history—2.6 million copies!

- I have had dinner with Chiang Kai-shek and Madame

Chiang, the secretary to the king of Denmark, and President Syngman Rhee, father of modern Korea.

- I sang "The Star-Spangled Banner" at the White House numerous times as a soloist for the Air Force Band and Singing Sergeants.
- I sold 100,000 copies of an album, *Howard Ruff Sings*, with the Osmond Brothers and the BYU Philharmonic and A Cappella Choir as my backup groups.
- I caught a piranha in the Amazon and ate it (poetic justice?).
- I've owned nine airplanes, and have logged 3,500 hours as "pilot in command."
- I was forced into bankruptcy in 1968 by a newspaper strike, and then paid off $500,000 (plus interest) in debts from which I had been legally discharged. It took me twelve years.
- Evelyn Wood personally taught me to read 3,000 words per minute, and I then developed the marketing and advertising that made her famous.
- I cruised the Mediterranean with Art Linkletter.
- I took over Madame Tussaud's Wax Works in London one night for a private party for my subscribers, and Kay and I flew to Ireland just to spend a weekend in a castle with Elizabeth Taylor. Unfortunately, she didn't show, so we spent a weekend in a castle in Ireland *without* Elizabeth Taylor.

Whenever I think I've accomplished a lot, I just remind myself that when Mozart was my age—he'd been dead for thirty-nine years.

Now let's get serious.

HOW I LEARNED WHAT NOT TO DO

I was born with a wooden spoon in my mouth. My mother was widowed when I was only six months old. We were poor but I didn't know it, because in the depths of the Great Depression everybody else was poor, too. We were actually too poor to afford a father. My mom literally took in sewing to feed me and my eleven-years-older brother, Jim. By the time I was nine years old, I knew what I wanted to be when I grew up: A writer? A financial adviser? A prophet of doom? None of the above! I was a really good boy soprano, and I knew I wanted to be a singer on Broadway or at the Met someday.

When I was a preadolescent during World War II, we lived in Reno, Nevada, and I became a member of the Victory Boys, a group of boy sopranos. We gave patriotic programs all over the state of Nevada. That's when I found what I loved the most in the whole world—applause!

When I was thirteen, we moved back to Oakland, where my voice changed abruptly from soprano to baritone, so at age sixteen, I joined a San Francisco musical theater company and also sang in San Francisco's famous opera clubs for ten dollars a night and tips. We would sing operatic arias and duets by request from 9:00 P.M. to 2:00 A.M. It was really just a smoke-filled bar, but I was doing what I loved to do.

When I was eighteen, my voice teacher told me she had arranged for a full-ride scholarship to the Curtis School of Music in Philadelphia. Curtis was considered on a par with Juilliard and could be a very important step on my road to the Met and Broadway, but when I told my mom, she threw a big monkey wrench into the works: "But you are supposed to go on a mission!" As a practicing Mormon family, it was expected that young men would volunteer to leave home for two years and teach the Gospel to potential converts, and I didn't want to go because I knew that my Curtis scholarship would be toast.

After a period of intense spiritual inquiry, I finally made the hard decision that unbeknownst to me would change the whole direction of my personal and professional life. I decided that if I served the Lord, He would take care of me, so with blind faith, I launched out into the dark and decided on the mission. They sent me to the heathens—Washington, D.C.—and not only did it jump-start my lifelong interest in government, economics, and politics, it was there that I first heard the Air Force Band and Singing Sergeants in a Sunday night concert on the Capitol steps, which would change my life forever. I was also befriended by the two senators from Utah, Arthur Watkins and Wallace Bennett (the father of Utah's present senator), and J. Willard Marriott Sr., of hotel fame. We had long discussions about life, business, and the issues of the day, and I began forming my economic, business, and political opinions. I attended the Missionary School of Hard Knocks, on thousands of doors, and learned one of the great lessons of life that every salesman and marketer must learn—how to live with rejection and failure and keep bouncing back day after day. It was a tough but immensely satisfying and character-building experience, and I regretted it when it was over.

After my mission, I went to BYU to continue my musical education. When I ran out of money after my junior year, I went back to San Francisco where my mother now lived, to make some money so I could go back to school, singing in the opera clubs by night and selling Chryslers by day. Then, unexpectedly, I was reclassified 1-A in the draft and ordered to report for induction into the army. I remembered the Air Force Singing Sergeants, called the Pentagon to get their phone number in

Washington, D.C., and was given the number of Col. George S. Howard, chief of bands and music for the Air Force, so I called him. He told me he had an opening for a new baritone soloist, but wouldn't be in California for six months, so I told him, "I'll audition in Washington next Wednesday."

I borrowed $150 from my big brother, flew to Washington, auditioned, got the job with a letter to prove it, and enlisted in the air force. After only three weeks of basic training, I was ordered to report to Washington to go with the Air Force Symphony on a tour of Iceland and Scandinavia as soloist and announcer, so I called the lovely Kay Felt in San Francisco and rather arrogantly informed her we would be married in Salt Lake City on the way to Washington the following Monday.

Fortunately, she couldn't think of any good reason why not, so we were married on schedule, and Kay Felt became Kay Felt Ruff (when she realized what her name would be, it almost killed the marriage). She has been the spiritual and nurturing center of my life and family, and our numerous kids (thirteen living, including five adopted as teenagers) and grandkids (sixty-nine at last count) all adore her—and so do I.

I traveled all over the world with the band, meeting and in some cases having dinner with such historical figures as Chiang Kai-shek, Syngman Rhee, and assorted prime ministers and royalty on three continents and twenty countries. We also toured in forty-eight states. I was having an amazing educational experience, while Kay was at home having babies.

But I wasn't really an absentee father. Being a Singing Sergeant was a government job, so when we weren't on tour (we were only gone about fifteen weeks out of the year), we only had to report for two hours a day for rehearsals, so I got a job with a stockbroker, continuing my economic and financial education, and spent a lot of time at home, helping Kay with the kids and learning to love fatherhood.

When my four-year hitch was up, we moved to Denver to work for my broker/employer, stumbled across Evelyn Wood Reading Dynamics, bought the Denver franchise, then the Bay area franchise, and launched my business career, teaching the world to read faster and more efficiently. I learned I had valuable gifts as a marketer, writer, and public speaker, but I was also laying the foundation for my first big learning experience—a business failure!

We had had eight glorious years, with more than 10,000 students in the San Francisco Bay area, and I wrote the ads and designed the marketing for all the nationwide franchises, and became the protégé of Evelyn Wood, who taught me how to read over 3,000 words-per-minute, a life-changing skill that has served me well ever since. We taught law students at the University of California and Stanford, high school and junior-high students, and businessmen how to read more rapidly and efficiently and both enjoy and absorb more from their reading. And as the money was rolling it, we spent it. We gave money to the Oakland Symphony, and I bought Kay a $1,000 designer dress so that when we had our picture on the society page at postconcert receptions, she would look great. In the meantime, our family was continuing to grow, and Kay bore more much-loved and much-wanted children.

However, I was making the biggest mistake of my life to that date, one that is the genesis of chapter 3, (although bigger mistakes would come later). Because I thought the gravy train would last forever, we didn't bother to accumulate any savings or cash reserves. We had good credit and used it. We spent our money as if there was no tomorrow, or, to be more accurate, I did. Kay expressed her concerns, which I discounted because I thought I knew better.

Then disaster struck. I had planned an eight-page advertising supplement to go into all of the Bay area newspapers one Sunday. On Friday night a wildcat strike hit all the Bay area papers, and the Sunday paper supplement was never distributed. I had spent $25,000 printing that supplement, which at the time seemed like all the money in the world, and we couldn't just keep them and use them at a later time because they were all geared toward specific demonstration meetings on specific dates at specific places all over the Bay area.

I was in deep trouble. I didn't have any cash reserves, accounts payable began to pile up, and we were up to our ears in hock and personal debt, and I was in arrears with my royalties. Finally the parent company, seeing an opportunity to grab off the business and resell it to someone else, abruptly canceled my franchise and notified the sheriff. My doors were locked and I was out of business. I went to work rich one day (I thought) and came home broke, which ruined my whole day.

This forced me into bankruptcy, but Kay and I, prompted by some ethical counseling by local church leaders, decided that even though we had filed bankruptcy, legally discharging half a million dollars in debt, we would not be right with our creditors and the Lord if we didn't someday pay it off. So I made perhaps the most important decision of my life—I would eventually pay off those debts, which meant I couldn't just get a J.O.B.; I had to become rich—again. That all happened in October 1968, and we had already been hit by a tragedy the previous June when our toddler, Ivan, was drowned in our swimming pool. This was a devastating year, but I now know that sometimes the healing and correcting spirit of God can only enter us through our gaping wounds, and this spiritual process had begun at Ivan's death when we had to decide what we really believed, so we were ready to make the spiritual, financial, and emotional commitment to pay off half a million dollars in debt. It took us twelve years to pay for that dead horse, but we did it! This lesson forty-five years ago has had a profound impact on this book, as it illustrates two of its most important principles, including the principle that *the first step in getting rich is simply to decide to do it,* which is what I did.

In the meantime, we had taken in a teenage foster son in the neighborhood who had become estranged from his family, and the word got around, so over the following years we took in more than eighteen of them, mostly teenagers, for varying lengths of time. We eventually adopted five of them.

I began my business comeback as a distributor in the multi-level sales organization for a major manufacturer of food supplements, the Neo Life Company, which is still in existence today and is one of the honorable survivors of the multilevel marketing business. I quickly became its largest distributor and won all of the company awards for performance, and began a lifelong obsession with keeping up with the research and development of nutritional supplements.

About this time, I began to worry about what I saw as a coming train wreck for the economy.

When I was in an airport, I saw a book whose title intrigued me, *How to Prepare for the Coming Crash* by Robert Preston. Thinking it was a way to stay safe if the airplane went down, I bought it to read on the plane, but that wasn't the crash it was talking about. Preston advocated investing in silver and gold as a hedge against an inflation-induced economic crash, and for the first time my stock-market-oriented brain began to turn in that direction. I began to study the fundamentals of Austrian economics and the inflation that would lead to economic troubles and a resurgence of gold, and began to worry about what I believed the government was doing to the economy with its inflationary policies.

I also became convinced that there was a real possibility of a deep recession that could possibly turn into a depression, characterized by high inflation and unemployment, so I became a vocal advocate of an emergency food-storage program as a kind of family-insurance program. After all, we had once lived on our stored food when the bottom had dropped out of our financial lives in 1968. This traditional Mormon practice grew not so much out of its theology as it did out of its nineteenth-century pioneer, self-sufficiency culture. It was not an apocalyptic practice, but a very practical one, designed for just the kind of circumstances we had to face, but this very prudent, riskless piece of financial advice planted the roots of what would someday be the cause of my near-universal bad press.

I wrote my first book, a very bad self-published book called *Famine and Survival in America*, not realizing how powerful words could be. Rather than a carefully reasoned discussion of why you ought to have a food-storage program as a conservative, prudent precaution against hard times for your family, it sounded more like a scream in the night. But to my amazement, as I began to do radio and TV shows to promote this self-published book, it caught on, as people were scared of what was happening in the world around them as inflation was cranking up.

In the book I promised to send a monthly update on the markets to book buyers, so I soon was sending out 5,000 monthly updates and going broke doing it. So I sold off my supplement distributorship to finance a for-pay newsletter, which I called *The Ruff Times* to a chorus of sardonic jeers, but my guts told me that name was right for our times, so I launched *The Ruff Times* newsletter in June 1975, forecasting rising inflation, a falling stock market, and rising gold and silver prices, and was I ever right. At the time, gold was only $110 an ounce and silver was under $2, and they had not yet begun the spectacular bull market that would take them to $850 and $50 respectively.

As the precious metals and *The Ruff Times* took off, I decided I needed to write a manual for new subscribers, because you couldn't reinvent the wheel for new subscribers every time you went to press. With no intention of publishing it as anything but a manual for new subscribers, I wrote *How to Prosper During the Coming Bad Years*, and self-published it in 1977. A member of my board of directors knew many New York publishers, so he persuaded me to go there to meet several of them, and four of them wanted to publish the book. I chose Times Books, a division of the *New York Times*, of all things, and Tom Lipscomb was president. Tom was a brilliant publisher and marketer who believed passionately in me and the book and shared my philosophy, and he and I made publishing history together—3 million copies!

By this time I had a syndicated TV talk show called *Ruffhou$e*, interviewing a lot of interesting guests, and I got a call from a radio syndicator who had been distributing the Ronald Reagan daily radio commentary. When Reagan decided to run for president, he gave up his radio show, so they asked me to fill that slot, as I was getting a lot of notoriety as the book hit the bestseller list and my TV show was gathering millions of viewers.

So I created a two-minute daily radio commentary, which eventually was on some three hundred stations, and *The Ruff Times* was on its way to the stratosphere—or so I thought!

As a public service to benefit from my high profile and high levels of trust from my like-minded subscribers, I founded RuffPAC, a political action committee, and Free the Eagle, a registered lobby in Washington, D.C., and began to fight for free market issues and free market–oriented candidates for public office. We were successful in some pretty important things, such as persuading President Reagan to get Stinger missiles to the Afghan rebels. This forced the Soviets to fly so high they wouldn't devastate the villages that were harboring the Mujahideen, and stalemated the war. When the body bags kept coming home and the Soviet Union was on the verge of bankruptcy trying to support their functional equivalent of our Vietnam, eventually Gorbachev withdrew the troops from Afghanistan, pulled back the Soviet army from their Iron Curtain satellites, stopped their financial support of Cuba, the Sandinistas in Nicaragua, and communist insurgent groups in Africa, and the Iron Curtain began to crumble. I honestly believe we had something to do with starting that whole process.

In any event, *The Ruff Times* had become a publishing phenomenon. *How to Prosper During the Coming Bad Years* was #1 or #2 on the hardcover bestseller list for months, and when the paperback came out a year later, it not only stayed on or near the top of the hardcover list, but was also #1 on the paperback list. It stayed high on both lists for two years.

Early on, the Prophet (sometimes spelled "Profit" by the media) of Doom title began to plague me. It seems that the hard-core "survivalists" were getting a lot of media attention. These extremists shared some of my economic views, but they believed that society would collapse completely, so they were building impregnable retreats in the mountains and buying lots of guns and storing food and hunkering down, waiting for the end—and I had a chapter in *How to Prosper During the Coming Bad Years* about the advisability of having a food-storage program as a riskless, prudent hedge against personal or public financial difficulties. There it was; guilt by association!

The simpleminded media saw me as a hook for critical stories about hard-core survivalists, and the Prophet of Doom title was forever attached to me, despite my protests. Heck, the "How to Prosper" in the title, which is not exactly an end-of-the-world idea, should have been a clue to them that they were wrong, but to no avail.

MY BIGGEST PROFESSIONAL FLOP?

The Y2K crisis! I believed that this was deadly serious and could have devastating effects on the economy, and said so in my letter, and even wrote a book on the subject. I was dead right about the seriousness of the problem, but for the only time in my life, I underestimated the willingness and the ability of government and industry to solve the problem in time to beat the deadline of January 1, 2000. Miraculously, they did fix it in time, due to the efforts of Sen. Bob Bennett of Utah and others, and on New Year's Day, 2000, when the dire consequences failed to materialize, I had egg all over my face, and that book became my first big publishing flop. It wasn't that I had not analyzed the problem properly; it was that I didn't believe that they would have the will and the smarts to fix it in time. I was wrong, big-time!

MY BIGGEST TRIUMPHS?

But it's not all bad. There were many triumphs, but two that stand out:

Way back in 1975 when I started publishing *The Ruff Times*, I foresaw the coming inflation that plagued us for the next seven years and analyzed, correctly, that it would cause a big boom in gold and silver and recommended gold when it was only $110 an ounce and silver when it was under $2. Gold subsequently went to $850 and silver to $50 for a few days, and I published a sell order when gold was $750 and silver at $35. This angered and offended my subscriber base, who were mostly "gold bugs," and they began deserting me as an apostate from the true religion of the "golden calf." For many years since then, gold stayed below $250, and silver under $5.

I turned bullish on the stock market in 1983, mostly because of Ronald Reagan, and stayed bullish for several years, and we did very well for my subscribers, but I started telling people to phase out of the stock market about six months before it peaked in March 2000 and called the market an "unsustainable mania and a bubble." This was right on the money, as March 2000 was the peak of the greatest bull market in history, and the beginning of the greatest bear market in history. I've been on the right side of that market ever since, keeping people out of it, and instead recommending thirty-year T-bonds and ten-year T-notes, where we had big profits in 2000–2003, and saved them untold millions of dollars.

In 1983, I was at the top of my popularity; my book was #1 on the bestseller lists in both hardcover and paperback and on its way to becoming the biggest financial bestseller of all time. My syndicated TV show *Ruffhou$e* was showing in 350 markets, and my two-minute daily radio commentary was on 300 stations. My newsletter *The Ruff Times* had more than 175,000 subscribers, and I thought I was a marketing genius, as all the direct-mail pieces I wrote worked. My Washington lobby, Free the Eagle, and RuffPAC, my political action committee, were real powers in Washington. I had access to President Reagan and any senator and congressman I wanted to talk to. I was famous, I was rich, and the world was my oyster. But just like the high-tech investors in March 2000, who thought they were great stock-pickers, it would in retrospect be the high-water mark of my professional and business life; it would be all downhill businesswise from there. Little did I realize that I wasn't the marketing genius I thought I was. I was just a very lucky guy with the right message at the right time, and if conditions changed much, I wouldn't be so smart. And conditions changed!

Ironically, even though I had campaigned vigorously for him and had warm personal relations with him, the election of Ronald Reagan was the beginning of a long, downhill slide for me. I had made my mark in the world by telling people how to prosper during the scary Jimmy Carter–induced inflation of the seventies. Ronald Reagan was my friend, and Jimmy Carter was my foil. Ronald Reagan and Paul Volcker's successful assault on the runaway inflation and interest rates of the late seventies made people less convinced we were facing some "coming bad years," and properly so, so my old message was less compelling. As I changed with the times and became properly bullish on America, the new message was less interesting than the old one, and media publicity was harder to come by.

During that years-long downhill slide I made a series of stupid mistakes that taught me most of what I know today, and laid the foundation for this safely-prosper or get-rich-surely book. I had learned how to make a fortune, and had done it twice, once in good times and once in bad times. Then I had learned how to *lose* a fortune, and had done that twice—also in good times and bad.

In retrospect, as I became a celebrity, my financial success and notoriety infected me with a bad case of "hubris"—the Greek word for "the arrogant pride of the gods." I unconsciously believed that I was so smart I could violate my own published rules with impunity and avoid the problems that would trip up lesser mortals, and my success wasn't teaching me a thing. Too often my operative principle was "do as I say, not as I do." Unfortunately, I was wrong—*really* wrong—which has cost me millions. Also, much of what I thought I knew that eventually turned out to be wrong came out of my successes.

One reason I felt driven to write this sometimes-embarrassing treatise is that I don't want my posterity to repeat all the foolish mistakes I will tell you about; my successes are nowhere near as instructive and helpful. If I can't pass on what I learned about the things that no longer work—or didn't work in the first place—some of my most valuable experiences would be wasted. I also want the "cathartic benefit" of publicly facing reality about myself and cramming a little humility down my unwilling throat. It will be too late when I am trying to explain my arrogant pride to God.

OLD FOGY WISDOM

This book could only be written by someone of my ripe years (sometimes I wish I was seventy-five again). I've observed the world of money through three serious recessions, three major bull and bear markets (including the late, lamented dot.com bubble of 1996–2000), the insane inflation of the seventies, a real estate boom and bust, a historic gold bull market and subsequent collapse, 14 children (five were adopted—we couldn't find homes for the other nine), 18 foster children, 69 grandchildren, and four great-grandchildren. I've made and lost two fortunes by making most of the stupid mistakes I describe here, been written off by Wall Street as a fringe character at times, but for a few glory years, I couldn't walk down any sidewalk in the Wall Street financial district without being recognized. For the last decade I've been laying low, laboring away in relative obscurity just publishing my newsletter on the Internet and germinating this book.

In short, in a financial world dominated by 20- and 30-something kids who weren't even stockbrokers during the last bear market in 1987, I'm one of a small clique of *real adults*—newsletter writers, financial publishers, analysts, and advisers—who are old enough to have been around since the sixties and seventies, through good times and bad. And for the most part Wall Street has not respected us, but that's OK because we don't have a lot of respect for many of them either, for reasons I have explained.

I'm also old enough and emotionally secure enough to admit my bloopers. In fact, that's part of what inspired this book. Like an old trailblazer, I want to mark the trail's pitfalls as warnings to those who follow after me, especially my numerous posterity.

Remember the old bridge builder:

> *An old man going the lone highway came at evening time cold and gray, to a chasm cold and wide and steep, with waters flowing cold and deep.*
>
> *The old man crossed in the twilight dim; the sullen stream held no fear for him. He stopped when safe on the other side and built a bridge to span the tide.*
>
> *"Old man," said a fellow pilgrim near, "you are wasting your time by building here. You've crossed the ravine deep and dark and wide. Why build this bridge at eventide?"*
>
> *The old man lifted his old gray head, "Good man, in the path I have trod," he said, "there follows after me today a youth whose feet must pass this way."*

I'm really building this bridge for him.

A REAL ADULT: I'VE BEEN THERE

I have been publishing *The Ruff Times* through thirty-two years of bull and bear markets, unlike most of the hot financial advisers and brokers during the late, lamented bull market, who are so young they weren't even brokers yet during the last bear market in 1987. They were the "invincible optimists" at the peak of the last bull market in the spring of 2000, when I was yelling at them to get out of the market. I think I am one of a handful of real adults in the Wall Street kindergarten with a long-range view of the world of money.

I can write to you about your concerns because there aren't many of you I can't identify with. No matter where you are in life, I've probably been there. Do you have a growing family? We have parented a ton of kids. I understand your fears for their future in an increasingly dangerous and volatile world, and know how hard it is to balance the search for wealth with the more important demands of family and church. I can relate.

Are you struggling with age and health problems? I've had cancer and a heart attack, although I'm in great health now for a man my age. I guess you couldn't kill me with an axe. I can relate.

Have you struggled to build a business, perhaps without success? I've started six, and three of them failed, and three of them succeeded. I can relate.

Do you have an extended family you love and worry about? So do I, in spades. There are eleven great-families in our posterity, and we have a real juggling act to stay close to them. I can relate.

Do you live in a big city? A small town? A rural area? I've

lived in all of them, from the San Francisco Bay area to a small Utah town with 2,000 souls. I can relate.

A single parent? My mother was one, so I grew up in a one-parent family. I can relate.

Are you retired, and trying to get by on your Social Security and inadequate interest on your savings? Well, I'm seventy-seven years old. I can relate.

Up to your ears in debt? Broke? Here I can *really* relate. When I was growing up, we were too poor to afford a father. I know what it's like to not have a car, or to be the last ones in our neighborhood to have an old black-and-white TV, and to live in second- or third-floor walk-ups. I've also lost two fortunes, one of them after we had just gone through the shock and pain of our toddler, Ivan, drowning in our pool.

I know what it's like to be a newly minted bankrupt standing in the ruins of a collapsed business.

I've been a small investor and a big investor. I've won big and lost big in business and the markets. I've been depressed and euphoric. I've loaned and borrowed. I've made every costly and stupid mistake there is. I've been there, and I can relate.

In short, I'm one of you. I'm not a twentysomething Wall Street hotshot in a $4,000 Brooks Brothers suit, detached from the realities you face every day, who thinks there is no real life west of the Hudson River. I'm just a regular family man who loves bass fishing, BYU football, the Utah Jazz, *Star Trek* on TV, directing my church choir, singing in, directing, and conducting Gilbert and Sullivan comic operas with the local opera company, dinner with Kay at the Outback or the Red Lobster, teaching a Sunday School class, off-the-wall humor, and movies that don't make me wade through garbage.

Prosperity or "real wealth" is within the reach of anyone—I promise! If you will do the things I have described here that the financially successful people do, prosperity or wealth is inevitable, and much will happen faster than you might think. However, it's not easy, because they both require big changes in your mental paradigm and attitudes and temperament.